Everyday STEWARDSHIP

REFLECTIONS FOR THE JOURNEY

Tracy Earl Welliver, MTS

Foreword by Leisa Anslinger

This book is dedicated to my
Bishop Ireton High School English teacher,
Bro. Rick Wilson, TOR,
who made me promise at graduation that he would see
a book of my writings one day in print.
It took 29 years, but a promise is a promise!
Thank you for all you taught me.

Contents

Acknowledgements

There are several people and communities that deserve my acknowledgement and sincere gratitude. Without them, there would be much less to reflect on and much less to inspire me. I have always told my children that we are the sum of our experiences. Those mentioned below have helped to create the person I am today, and in turn, made this book possible.

SO THANK YOU...

To my Mom & Dad, both deceased, for always believing in me and making me feel like anything was possible in life.

To those involved many decades ago in Youth Encounter in the Diocese of Arlington, Virginia. These retreats over 30 years ago changed my life.

To the Oblates of St. Francis DeSales, who taught me that holiness is everyday living and not something to be separate from our common experience.

To Fr. Robert Lange, who died in May 2015, for being my guide and friend when I was becoming a young man. You showed me what a priest should be and I will always cherish the fact that we reconnected just months before your passing. Please put in a good word for me with the Boss.

To the community of Saint Pius X Catholic Church in Greensboro, NC, for taking me in as a child and helping to form me into a man. At SPX, I learned not only what stewardship meant, but I witnessed its transformative power. Monsignor Marcaccio, thank you for pushing me to always be better tomorrow than I am today.

To Pat Spivey, my friend, for taking this stewardship journey with me and always dreaming with me about what could be.

To Liturgical Publications, for making my professional dreams come true.

To Carin Winghart, for believing in me and being my source of confidence when I was unsure of what could be achieved. I owe so much to you.

To my children, Nathan, Sarah Kate, and Zac, for being three of the greatest gifts in my life. You are a constant source of inspiration. I love you.

To my wife, Mariann, for simply loving me, for being my personal proofreader, and for always being there on this crazy journey in good times and in bad. I love you.

To my Lord and Savior, Jesus Christ, for calling me to this wonderful journey. You never forced me to do anything, but who could really say "No."

Foreword

When I was first introduced to stewardship as a way of life, it seemed pretty straightforward: recognize that everything is a gift from God, grow in gratitude for the gift, and live more generously as a result. Of course, as I began applying the principles of stewardship to my life, I found that it is not quite as straightforward as I initially believed. The reality is, living as a good steward is a deep and wonderful way of life, but there are many obstacles we must face if we intend to live in this manner.

The United States bishops name some of the obstacles in living as a steward in the introduction to their pastoral letter on stewardship, *Stewardship: A Disciple's Response*. "Although religious faith is a strong force in the lives of many Americans, our country's dominant secular culture often contradicts the values of the Judeo-Christian tradition. This is a culture in which destructive "isms" – materialism, relativism, hedonism, individualism, consumerism – exercise seductive, powerful influences." For myself, I cannot always blame the influence of the surrounding culture when I am tempted to ignore Christ's call to discipleship. I know in my heart the real temptation lies within: the tendency to take the many blessings of life for granted; the temptation to approach life from a perspective of entitlement rather than gratitude; the tendency to be selfish, or simply lazy in my spiritual life, resulting in life turned in on myself rather than pointed toward God and others.

Living and growing as disciples and stewards calls us to be attentive to such temptations and to overcome them, to take the Gospel call of Christ to heart. The more we hear the message of stewardship and reflect on it, the more likely we will be to recognize and be grateful for the many gifts we have been given: our lives, talents, time, resources, relationships and faith, for example. In developing attentive eyes, ears, and hearts, gratitude will become our first response rather than an afterthought. From gratitude does come generosity, for many of us very slowly, with many moments of failure along the way.

"Everyday stewardship" implies that this is a practical way of life that can impact the daily situations of our lives. Let me share one example of how I have experienced such everyday stewardship in my own life. In my childhood and adolescence, I thought my mother was generous to a fault. We had little money and moved often as a result of my father's work. My mother, a Catholic school cafeteria manager, always seemed to have someone who needed her help: an older woman who needed transportation to the grocery, doctor, and so on; co-workers who needed help in pulling off large family gatherings; a fledgling soup kitchen that began by offering Thanksgiving lunch to the poor in our area. At the time, my teenage self saw the good my mother was doing, but wondered why she was so generous. It was not until I was a mother myself that I began to understand. I know my mother would not have used the word "stewardship" to describe what she was doing, and yet it is exactly what it was. My mother understood that, in spite of having little money or physical security, she was blessed. And in recognizing our blessings, she responded in faith, and in gratitude. She trusted God above all else, and taught my brother and I to do the same. Not only this, my mother had reflected on the gifts she had been given: patience, the ability to organize large events, skill in cooking, in quantities I still cannot imagine. She understood that she was called to give her gifts and talents and to do so with a sense of joy.

I asked my mother about all of this one time in her later years. By then, my mother was living with my husband, children and me, and our parish had invited a stewardship speaker to address us at the end of Sunday Mass. On the way home, my mother said she had appreciated the speaker's message, and then shared her recognition of her own life of faith and giving in what she had heard. We talked about how living as a follower of Jesus changes over time, as does the ways in which we may give. Mom said, "I never had much money to give, but I always tried to give of my time when I could." With that, we began to share stories of my memories of her giving when I was younger, and how I didn't understand for quite some time why she gave as generously as she did. I teased her about one particularly frustrating day with one of the women she helped with errands. She smiled and said, "I am happy you get it now," and in that simple conversation, I realized how much she taught me through the way she lived her life, simply and with purpose. She lived as a steward every day.

I am sure my mother would have appreciated Tracy Earl Welliver's reflections on everyday stewardship, as do I. I find his examples and insights inspiring, and practical. Tracy recognizes that embracing stewardship and growing in this profound way of life is a dynamic process. His reflections help us to bring our faith to our daily lives, stretching us and challenging us to not be satisfied with the way things are in our lives, gently applying the principles of stewardship in ways that encourage our prayerful reflection and renewed commitment to Christ and to the steward's way. Tracy's reflections remind me of the way my mother lived as a steward, with practical commitment, every day.

One of the greatest gifts in this book, I believe, is the way we are led to reflect on familiar passages of Scripture, bringing them to life, and bringing the message to our daily lives. I plan to leave the page open at our family table, so that we can think about the passage and Tracy's reflection together. His ideas for response are simple and yet will truly make a difference in our lives of prayer and action, linking our faith to our living in practical ways. The reflection questions take this to a deeper level, inviting growth by imbedding this trustful, generous way into our consciousness. The doodle box will serve as a place for personal reflection and as an open-ended journal through which we may apply the lessons in our lives, through our notes, sketches and stories.

I am grateful to Tracy Earl Welliver for being such a good steward of his talents and insights in the collection of reflections that follows. I pray we all may continue to embrace Christ's call to love and serve, as stewards, every day.

—Leisa Anslinger

Charting the Course

The Impact of Stewardship

One day, many years ago, I was walking through the church of my parish, Saint Pius X Catholic Church in Greensboro, NC, with my pastor at the time, Fr. Frank Connolly. I have no recollection of what we were talking about or why we were even walking in the church. What I do remember is a man named Cal came up to us and spoke to Fr. Frank. "The kneeler on a pew up in the front of the church is broken," Cal said with a tone that showed he knew at least someone needed to know. I am sure he assumed that the pastor was the most logical person to tell. Fr. Frank's response was one I will remember as long as I live. Fr. Frank said, "Then you should go fix it."

I had no idea what to make of such a response. I knew that he was not being rude, since I could not conceive of this old and gentle priest with a white as snow beard ever being rude. Of course, it was Cal's response that informed me of what Fr. Frank really meant. Cal said he would be back before the weekend Masses with the tools to fix it. Surprisingly, except maybe not to Fr. Frank, Cal would fix many things at the church for the next several years. He, in essence, became the church handyman. All this occurred because his pastor reminded him of a great truth: this church belonged to us all, including Cal.

That was the beginning of my education in stewardship. I had two theology degrees but stewardship was never really a topic. I knew the term in respect to the environment, but not in terms of discipleship. Fr. Frank taught Cal and me a valuable lesson that day about what it means to be a steward.

Mature Discipleship

The United State Bishops' pastoral letter, *Stewardship: A Disciple's Response*, begins with three main convictions. Simply put,

1. We are called to become mature disciples who respond to the call of Jesus Christ regardless of the cost.
2. This leads to a way of life, not a series of activities or events.
3. This way of life is transformational.

I have spoken all over the US and in other parts of the world and too often I notice that stewardship becomes a yearly calendar of events that have as their centerpiece a ministry fair and commitment card. Those things are important in any parish promoting stewardship, but they are not stewardship. Also, very often without an underlying spirituality and philosophy of living, those things don't transform people. Transformation comes about when a person embraces the convictions listed above. When more and more people in a parish community are transformed, then the parish itself can be transformed. It is a simple equation, but not an easy goal to achieve.

The goal is not easy because it is not always easy to be a mature disciple. There are times when it seems much easier to say "no" to the call of Jesus Christ. We find ourselves lazy, scared, apathetic, ignorant, or selfish. We want God to respond to us when we call, but when the call comes from Heaven itself, Earth can look much too comfortable at times. But that really is immaturity of spirit and faith. We might respond like a child because we see things like a child. And one of the greatest mistakes we can make in life is thinking that as we grow older maturity is something that just happens naturally. Parents all around the world can assure us this is not true in any aspect of human life. Faith is no different.

In the Catholic Church, and in many other Christian communities, we have not always done such a good job of ongoing catechesis and spiritual development. Thankfully, with the work of people like Sherry Weddell (Intentional Discipleship) and Matthew Kelly (Dynamic Catholicism), there is a strong movement among American Catholics to take more seriously our baptismal call. In places like New Zealand, the recently named Cardinal John Dew of Wellington has embraced stewardship as a pathway to a more vibrant Church where people feel they truly belong. Church communities in Australia are working hard to implement stewardship principles and demonstrate to an increasingly secular society that disciples of Jesus Christ are still very relevant.

I am not a pessimist about the current state or the future of the Church. There is no doubt we have had a troubling few decades, but the Holy Spirit is moving in a profound way in parish community after parish community. But the reality in building a better reality is that a Church **community** is made up of **individuals** like you and me that must be committed to a new way of life. We must truly embrace transformation and allow good stewardship to permeate our entire being. It is easier to acknowledge the most obvious of God's gifts in our life: our loved ones, our belongings, and our own lives. But we must constantly reflect on our everyday lives to see how God calls us in not so obvious of ways. Mature disciples are called to be *Everyday Stewards*.

Becoming an Everyday Steward

How does Jesus Christ call to us in the everyday circumstances of our life? If we are people outwardly active in our faith we can see God working in our lives at monumental moments: the birth of a child, the death of a loved one, or the offer of a new job. Because we at least attend Mass most Sundays and pray before meals and bedtime, we have alerted our senses enough to see God as present in major life moments. What about hearing the voice of God in the ordinary, mundane, and even boring moments of our lives? That can be a different story. However, finding God there is at the core of real transformation as a faithful steward.

If we believe that all comes from God as gift and that we are to cultivate it and return it with increase to God, then we mean ALL. When we talk about gifts of time, talent, and treasure, we often focus too heavily on that which we offer to our parish community or favorite charities. But ALL means ALL. The time I spend at the parish working with children in a faith formation class is very important, but so is the time I spend at home alone in the quiet. Giving my talent by singing in the church choir is definitely good stewardship, but so is the making of a sandwich for a child's lunch. The money I take out of my wallet and place in the collection basket belongs to God, but so does the rest of the money that goes back into my pocket. When we begin to understand that my life is permeated with all the gifts God has given me, then we can begin to be mindful of God in all our circumstances. Suddenly, God is with me at every turn and I have the opportunity to be a good steward throughout the entire day.

Can you see how this understanding can transform a person? As my own understanding of stewardship developed, I began seeing my children differently. Before, they were my kids. It was my job to be the best parent I could be. They were gifts from God, but they were mine. Then I began to see them not as mine but God's. They were given to me, but not forever, so they were not in the same sense mine. They belonged to God. It was no longer my job to be a good parent, it was my calling to help them become the best people possible and impart to them a love for Jesus, because I was going to give them back someday. Furthermore, parenting became less about the big stuff and more about the everyday encounters. I realized that God was there with us not only for the triumphs and disappointments of childhood, but also when the request came to shoot some hoops in the driveway. I always saw the importance of being a disciple of Jesus Christ in my life on a daily basis, but now I saw the importance of being a disciple in my everyday life. Stewardship is not just about living a way of life every day, it is about normal EVERYDAY LIFE!

Characteristics of an Everyday Steward

When giving talks on this subject, I share 6 primary characteristics of an Everyday Steward. These characteristics are necessary to emulate on the way to becoming an Everyday Steward, but they are also fruits of living as an Everyday Steward. A great discussion in a small group using this book could be what additional characteristics would you add to the list. For our purposes here, we will focus on 6 in the reflections.

1. Mindful

How often does a moment pass by and we barely recall what happened? People tell me they often can't remember the experience of eating lunch, or sitting at a traffic light, or listening to music. They are there, but they are preoccupied with all the stuff in their brains. Their ability to live in the moment is hindered by the baggage of the past and the expectation of the future.

I am reminded of the story in John's Gospel of Mary anointing the feet of Jesus with expensive oil and then Judas' objection. Jesus reminds him that His time is short and He will not always be there with them in body. The reality is time is always short and a moment passed will never return. If we are not aware of the sensations and reality of the moment, we miss a chance to hear the call of Jesus and we miss a chance to really acknowledge the gifts we have been given.

All moments of life offer chances to give thanks to God, to hear His still small voice, and to reflect on the goodness of all that has been given. Brushing our teeth, eating a salad, feeling the warmth of sunlight, and watching people pass by can all be opportunities for stewardship reflection. Unless we live each day mindfully, those opportunities just will vanish forever. Plato said, "The unexamined life is not worth living." Now I wouldn't speak that strongly, but if we are going to draw the most meaning out of our lives, we must allow God to permeate all of it. That means paying attention to the Divine in even the most mundane of situations.

2. Prayerful

Living as an everyday steward is not easy, but without prayer, it is impossible. We are called to pray in many ways since a relationship has many facets. Sometimes we do the talking, and sometimes we are listening. Other times we are just resting in God's presence. In prayer we petition, we give thanks, and we give glory and praise. We offer our emotions of joy, fear, sadness, anger, and uncertainty. Our goal is to realize God is with us constantly and we need to be mindful we are always in the presence of the Divine.

I often suggest 2 daily prayers to assist us in living this way of life. In the morning, use the words of St. Francis de Sales as a start to the day: *"Call to mind that the day now beginning is given to you in order that you may work for Eternity, and make a steadfast resolution to use this day for that end."* Take a moment to reflect on these words and then offer the day to God. Ask for the strength to make the day count for something. One of the greatest abuses of God's gifts is the wasting of time. Be open to the many moments of the day as potential callings. Be the difference in someone's life this day. Take the chance to bring someone closer to God today, for what happens today, might last for all eternity.

Then at night use the words of St. Ignatius of Loyola:

> Take, Lord, and receive all my liberty,
> my memory, my understanding,
> and my entire will,
> all I have and call my own.
> You have given all to me.
> To you, Lord, I return it.
> Everything is yours;
> do with it what you will.
> Give me only your love and your grace,
> that is enough for me. Amen.

Sometimes called The Radical Prayer, the Suscipe is in many ways the ultimate stewardship prayer. Its focus is on everything belonging to God. It speaks beautifully of how we can give back everything to the one who created it and all that remains is the love and grace of God, which is always more than enough.

With this as an end of the day reflection, we are to also pause and reflect on how we have not given all to God throughout that day. When did I miss a chance to encounter Jesus in another? Where did I fail to be the best disciple and steward I can be? The prayer then becomes a statement of resolve for the next day to come. We pray always to be better tomorrow than we are today. Through God, this prayer can become reality.

3. Grateful

How can one acknowledge the presence of God throughout all aspects of life and not give thanks? The sheer magnitude of the gift of life and all in it should move us to gratitude. Unfortunately, we too often forget to be grateful because of selfishness, self-centeredness, or not being mindful of the reality of our situation. But not only should we give thanks, we are called to give thanks.

Thanksgiving changes us. Elie Wiesel has said, "For me, every hour is grace. And I feel gratitude in my heart each time I can meet someone and look at his or her smile." He survived a Nazi concentration camp! For Christians, being grateful allows others to see more clearly a joy of the Lord in us. When we focus on our blessings and consistently give thanks for them, we become transformed.

In stewardship, we are called to receive all from God with a grateful heart. We often hear the slogan, "An Attitude of Gratitude." The key here is to be grateful for the little things along with the obvious gifts we receive. Be thankful for the hands that touch a loved one's face, the gift of music we hear on the car radio, and the bees that fly about our head because they pollenate the earth around us. Don't let a day go by without finding things for which to give thanks to God. God calls you to gratefulness, not because he needs your thanks, but because of the transformative power of being grateful.

4. Gracious

The word gracious means so many things: kind, pleasant, courteous, merciful, and compassionate. It comes from Latin, meaning "good will." In the Gloria we recite or sing at Mass, we speak of "peace to men of good will." We lift up people who are of good will, gracious, because they are truly touched by grace and they serve as channels of that grace for others.

Hospitality is a fruit of being gracious. It is interesting what happens when we practice hospitality. When we are hospitable to others, we welcome Jesus into our midst, and we also become Jesus for that person. It truly is the saying, "The Jesus in me loves the Jesus in you."

Stewardship principles dictate that we must treat all of creation in a gracious manner. In everyday stewardship spirituality, we constantly are called on throughout the day to be gracious. To be welcoming and hospitable not only works to mold our own attitude towards the world, but it assists in the evangelization of that world. Practice your graciousness and see how people around you are more willing to hear what you have to share with them.

5. Committed

To succeed at something we need to persevere, especially if the task is not easy. Being a good steward often runs counter to the prevailing culture of the day. More importantly, it can go against our human nature. We feel our wants and needs more strongly than those of others. However, when we make a commitment to this way of life, not only do we get ourselves back up after we fall, but we know that as our lives are transformed, it becomes easier to think of God and others over ourselves.

In Matthew 16, Jesus asks us to pick up our cross and follow Him. We know this path is not easy. In Matthew 19, Jesus tells us to sell all we have, to give freely to the poor, and follow Him. It is a message of the totality of our lives belonging to God in a stewardship way of life. No one can live this life without strong commitment. It would be like trying to lose weight by dieting only twice a week. We are either in or out.

However, just like in dieting, no matter how committed we are we can count on failing along the way. The difference is knowing that failing is not the end. I recall seeing a poster where it showed two ways of looking at life. One way saw a fork in the road with one route leading to the prize, the other route leading to failure. The second way shows only one route that really leads to the prize. It is a winding road where failure happens over and over, but due to commitment, it ended with the prize.

Of course, in order to stay committed, one needs to take advantage of the assistance God provides. Prayer, study, scripture, and sacraments are all important tools at our disposal for the journey. Also, if these things are experienced in the context of community we will be that much stronger. An everyday steward is never alone.

6. Accountable

Here is the characteristic that seems to be the stumbling block for many, but in some ways, it may be the most important. This characteristic speaks to the value of community and the role we are called to play in each other's lives. Unless we are held accountable and understand the need to hold ourselves accountable, we can too easily fall into the trap of fooling ourselves. We start to believe we are someone we are not. Additionally, we can find ourselves on a slippery slope to a loss of integrity.

When I talk about the role a parish community can have in calling people to accountability, I often get pushback. Some think that the community can come off sounding critical or unloving. But I would argue that saying nothing to a person who has wandered off the path is the opposite of love. Not only should we be accountable to each other, we are responsible for each other. The Church is not a civic organization that one chooses to join and perhaps even pay dues. It is a family.

The well-respected author and businessman, Stephen Covey, said, "Accountability breeds response-ability." When we are willing to hold each other accountable, we create an environment where stewardship responses come more naturally. Spiritual direction, prayer groups, etc. can be great aides to help one stay on the stewardship path. Movements like Cursillo are built on the supposition that we are members of the Body of Christ, therefore, not alone.

If you are not currently involved in a group inside or outside of a faith community where people can truly lean on one another and speak truth in love, seek out friends in faith and ask them to journey with you.

Some will ask immediately after reading the list of six characteristics if there are additional ones to add to the list. That's fair. What a great discussion to have in a stewardship committee or prayer group using the book. This isn't science, so I encourage you to explore the question. Some possible characteristics like trusting, loving, and peaceful are not included because either I view them as fruits of the six or characteristics that already exist as normative for even the most cultural of Christians. It strikes me as too obvious to say an everyday steward should be kind or loving. Hopefully, we are these things by nature of being human.

Of course, the most glaring omission from the list is generous. How could I leave out generosity!?! Let me explain. Stewardship is almost by definition generosity. Giving and the act of giving is what stewardship is essentially. For people who find the word stewardship a stumbling block, generosity might be a decent synonym. In fact, in Spanish there is no good word for stewardship. To explain the concept to a Spanish-speaking person I will use the concept of generosity. Therefore, by not having it in the list, I feel I have chosen not to use a word to describe itself.

How to Use This Book

The beauty in possessing a book is that it is yours! I may have written the content of this book, but after it leaves me and enters into your hands, it is yours. I say this because I want to encourage you to consider reading this book in many different ways. My library has many reflection books in it and I have never used two of them in the same manner. However, I do have a few suggestions to help you get the most out of the content contained here. Let's first talk briefly about the content.

The reflections contained here were largely written during the B cycle of Sunday readings so they often speak to the themes contained in those Scripture selections. A few verses of scripture are included for each reflection and I have tried to include only the most pertinent content. You may choose to use a Bible at times to understand the full setting of the verses. The reflections are also organized loosely by using the 6 characteristics of an everyday steward. This was more of an editorial necessity so the reader could more easily use the book. Many reflections could have landed in several different characteristic sections.

After each reflection you will find an idea that might help to reinforce the message of the piece or might challenge you to go outside yourself for personal and spiritual growth. Some suggestions are harder to do than others, but you will almost certainly find new perspectives and develop spiritually if you are willing to attempt the response indicated. Of course, they are only "ideas" and you may have your own ideas of how to make a response. I just know from decades as a catechetical leader that if people are asked to respond in some manner to the message presented they are more likely to internalize the message.

Finally, at the end of each of my written reflections, you have a question on which to reflect. You will notice that often times the question asks for you to call to mind 3 of something. This is purposeful. I have found that most people can easily come up with an answer to a question such as, "Who is one person that needs your prayers?" Asking for 2 people does make one think a bit more. But usually, asking for 3 of something really stretches the mind and the heart. You certainly can always answer with 1 response, but I have constructed the questions so that you are stretched and you really spend time thinking about each question.

Accompanying that question is what I call a doodle box. This is your space for anything. Respond how your personality leads you to do so. I am a writer but I cannot journal. No matter how many people tell me about the fruits of journaling, I cannot do it. Writing to myself? No way! Writing to God? I'd rather have a chat over a glass of wine in a quiet room. So, this doodle box can be a space for writing, drawing, scribbling, etc. You can paste pictures there. You can write reminders of how to concretely respond to the question. Please do not put any rules on yourself. Hopefully this book can really make a difference in the way you view stewardship and live your life, but if you think reading it requires you to do something you cannot do, then it will sit on a shelf forever.

Now here are some suggestions on how one person or a group of people could use the book, outside of the obvious:

1. Everyday Stewardship Prayer Groups
One of the characteristics of an everyday steward is accountability. Meeting weekly to share with one another the struggles and successes of living a stewardship way of life can go a long way in promoting spiritual growth and maturity. Participants can share with the group their experiences of following through with some of the response ideas and their answers to the reflection questions. The group could focus on 2 or 3 reflections a week. Also, the group could spend time going through the 6 characteristics of an everyday steward found in the front of the book, sharing successes and struggles with each one that week.

2. Personal Growth Challenge

You could commit to reading each reflection, acting on the response idea, and reflecting on the questions. I guarantee that you would be a different person after reading over 60 reflections and completing all the activities. I know just writing all the content has changed me!

3. Bible Study

I will not pretend that by any stretch of the imagination this book is truly a Bible study. However, you can use it to begin a habit of reading and reflecting on scripture if you don't do so already.

4. Stewardship Committee Reflections

Using a reflection to begin or end stewardship committee meetings would be a great way of helping the committee understand that stewardship is about much more than ministry fairs and commitment cards. In fact, it could help them see why those things are so important in the first place: because they lead to a greater reality. Keywords are printed vertically on each right page to allow you to find a reflection quickly that meets your needs.

There are many ways to use this book, but the important thing is that you use the book. Don't let it just sit on a shelf. It was meant to inspire, inform, and evangelize, and was written in a way so that anyone could benefit from its content.

Thank you for considering embarking upon this journey. This might be a beginning for you or just another leg on an already powerful spiritual expedition. Either way, keep in mind God is there every day in the smallest of life's moments. Together, as everyday stewards, let us strive to be better today than we were yesterday, and better tomorrow than we are today. Let us be mature disciples who respond daily to the call of Jesus. We will be transformed, and our parish communities will be transformed as well.

Beginning the Journey

The Heart of Stewardship

While they were eating, he took bread, said the blessing, broke it, and gave it to them, and said, "Take it; this is my body." Then he took a cup, gave thanks, and gave it to them, and they all drank from it. He said to them, "This is my blood of the covenant, which will be shed for many. Amen, I say to you, I shall not drink again the fruit of the vine until the day when I drink it new in the kingdom of God."

—Mark 14:22-25

What else is there to give when one has already given away one's body and one's life? What more can one say or do to demonstrate love for another when all one has has been given to another? This total giving of self to loved ones cannot be trumped by flowery words or material gifts that are fleeting. This is the ultimate in love. This is the love Jesus had for us on the way to His Passion, at the institution of the Holy Eucharist. This is the love He has for us daily in the celebration of the Mass on altars in every church, in every city, in every nation on earth. No one can give more. No one can ask for more. This is the true heart of Christian stewardship.

If you take the time to gaze upon your God in the simplest of forms, and begin to reflect on what has actually taken place with bread and wine becoming the presence of the Divine, then you can begin to understand true humility, sacrifice, and love. And when you have the privilege to take that Real Presence into your body at the meal where you are an honored guest, you become one with the One who is the embodiment of stewardship. Then, you must ask the question of yourself, "How can I even begin to reflect the love that I have encountered at this feast?" The answer is you can begin with the simple actions of the day: where will you go, whom will you meet, and in what work will you partake? Jesus Christ has shown that the greatest gift ever given can be disguised in this world in a piece of bread. By joining your body to His, He can now transform human hearts, not by grand acts, but by everyday acts, by everyday people, practicing Everyday Stewardship.

IDEA FOR RESPONSE

Do you know someone who needs a ride to Mass, or someone whom you have seen frequently attending Mass alone? Consider making someone a "Mass buddy" so that person can more fully experience the heart of stewardship.

TAKE TIME TO REFLECT

What are 3 things in my routine of preparing for Mass that I can change to make my experience more meaningful and fruitful?

Striving for Maturity

Therefore, let us leave behind the basic teaching about Christ and advance to maturity, without laying the foundation all over again: repentance from dead works and faith in God, instruction about baptisms and laying on of hands, resurrection of the dead and eternal judgment. And we shall do this, if only God permits.

—Hebrews 6:1-3

The US Bishops' pastoral letter on stewardship was published in 1992 as a challenge to embrace a way of life with the "power to change how we understand and live out our lives." It calls us to a mature discipleship that requires a decision to follow Jesus Christ no matter the cost. However, this notion brings to mind the words of Maya Angelou, "Most people don't grow up. Most people age. They find parking spaces, honor their credit cards, get married, have children, and call that maturity. What that is, is aging!"

Maturity is also a notion that we sometimes have failed to understand in the Church. The years of talking about teenagers becoming adults in the Church at Confirmation certainly didn't help. Being older certainly doesn't mean one is necessarily mature. Age and experience come our way whether we want it to or not. What we learn from the passage of time is what brings about maturity.

Mature disciples come in all ages really. To test maturity one simply needs to ask the question given to us in the challenge of the Bishops' pastoral letter: "Will I follow Jesus Christ no matter the cost?" One cannot grow in a sense of stewardship if he or she is always "counting the cost." Think of children's reactions to requests of their time and effort: "That's not fair!" "I don't feel like it!" "How come I have to do it?"

If we seriously follow Jesus and become good observers of our lives, we realize that every day there are costs: some days less than others, and some days much more. A mature Everyday Steward will hit those challenges head on with trust in the Lord. It does become easier, though, as maturity grows because, as the US Bishops point out, to lead this way of life transforms a person. The great promise in this is that transformed people begin to transform the world around them. Who doesn't want that? ("Immature people, of course," said the still, small voice.)

IDEA FOR RESPONSE
Find a good book, magazine, or video to read or watch that educates you on some aspect of the Catholic Church you know little about.

TAKE TIME TO REFLECT

At what times in my life do I find a mature response to God's call the hardest? What steps can I take to move toward a greater maturity?

Answering the Question of "Why?"

He willed to give us birth by the word of truth that we may be a kind of first fruits of his creatures. Know this, my dear brothers: everyone should be quick to hear, slow to speak, slow to wrath, for the wrath of a man does not accomplish the righteousness of God. Therefore, put away all filth and evil excess and humbly welcome the word that has been planted in you and is able to save your souls. Be doers of the word and not hearers only, deluding yourselves. For if anyone is a hearer of the word and not a doer, he is like a man who looks at his own face in a mirror. He sees himself, then goes off and promptly forgets what he looked like.

—James 1:18-24

Stewardship must never become reduced to simply ministry fairs, commitment cards, and stewardship directories. These are tools by which we learn how to practice our stewardship, but they are not stewardship in of themselves. All actions of giving or sharing should flow from the mature heart of person, mindful of the reasons why these actions are important at all. If we lose sight of the motivations for our actions, we risk becoming a bell without a ring or a piano with no tones. The answer should always be on the tip of our tongues and the forefront of our minds to the question: WHY?

Too often we forget that the activities of parish stewardship exist only to lead us into a way of living. Every Sunday is Commitment Sunday. Every day there is a call upon us to respond. And without the answer to "why," we become the sum of things we do, rather than the love and grace we hold in our hearts.

So why do we share our time, talent, and treasure? What does it matter? We can give the simplistic answer, "Because God asks us to." But since we are called to be mature in our discipleship, then the question that demands an answer is, "Why does he ask these things of us?" And there lies the crux of the matter. We are called to do these things, so that we may bear witness to the reality of the transforming power of Jesus Christ, so that others may come to follow him as well.

It is great to have more money in the collection, and more hands to share the load. But at the end of the day, it is about more than making our parish lives better. It is about leading people to heaven. If we can understand that, then every day becomes an important day for stewardship, and Everyday Stewards can help God transform all those around them.

IDEA FOR RESPONSE
Make a list of 3 things you have done for someone and the reasons why God called you to do those things.

TAKE TIME TO REFLECT

Do I understand the specific reasons why God has called me to offer my time, talent, or treasure to my parish or someone in my parish?

The Things We Do

"Do you not believe that I am in the Father and the Father is in me? The words that I speak to you I do not speak on my own. The Father who dwells in me is doing his works. Believe me that I am in the Father and the Father is in me, or else, believe because of the works themselves. Amen, amen, I say to you, whoever believes in me will do the works that I do, and will do greater ones than these, because I am going to the Father. And whatever you ask in my name, I will do, so that the Father may be glorified in the Son."

—John 14:10-13

A primary conviction of the Bishops' pastoral letter on stewardship is that stewardship is about a way of life, not a series of actions. What does a "way of life" mean? Stewardship aside, I wonder to myself how often in various areas of my life I have fallen into a pattern of actions where I don't take time to reflect on what I am doing. The process of moving from just actions toward a way of life begins with the answer to a short but sometimes difficult question: WHY?

It is easy to say that a food collection, the volunteering of some hours of service, or the phone call to a friend in need is a good thing. All people of good will are called to do things like these. The "why" we do these things is Jesus. However, sometimes we fall into a trap where actions become unreflective habits, even though they are good habits.

There is an impact on others that is so meaningful when we share our time, talent, and treasure, but there is also an impact on us. That impact becomes that much greater when we take time to reflect on why we are doing something. Our streams of generosity can become roaring rivers that have the possibility of changing the entire landscape around them.

IDEA FOR RESPONSE

Decide to give money or food to a drive or agency. As you are in the action of doing so, reflect on why God has called you to do this and how it will help someone in need.

TAKE TIME TO REFLECT

What are 3 things I did in the past year out of generosity that I didn't even pause to think about why I was doing them?

WAY OF LIFE

Be Mindful

The 1st Characteristic of an Everyday Steward

A Really Happy Meal

So whether you eat or drink, or whatever you do, do everything for the glory of God. Avoid giving offense, whether to Jews or Greeks or the church of God, just as I try to please everyone in every way, not seeking my own benefit but that of the many, that they may be saved.

—1 Corinthians 10:31-33

Being everyday stewards means to be mindful of the gifts God has given us in all aspects of life and to act in ways that give glory to Him. This is easy when we look at the more profound actions in our lives, such as participating in a parish service project or raising money for the poor. But God is just as present to us in the ordinary and everyday aspects of our daily lives.

Paul wrote to the Corinthians, "Whether you eat or drink, or whatever you do, do everything for the glory of God." Of course, Paul never visited a McDonald's! But even though it may seem like a stretch to the common man, by being mindful of where we are, whom we are with, and what we are doing, a McDonald's experience can give glory to God.

I have a photo of my oldest child, decked out with his cowboy hat and sitting in a booster, having his first Happy Meal at McDonald's. That was over 15 years ago and on that day I probably wasn't thinking much about giving God the glory. However, I reflect on that event and realize how much it was a celebration of life and the good gifts God had given me. If I were to be there today, I would focus more and take in the surroundings, and really accept God into that moment. I would be mindful of each bite we both took and the expressions on his face. I would take note of the others around us and wonder if the joy we were experiencing at the time was noticeable and if that joy brought God into their lives just a little on that day. After all, even though it is a clever marketing scheme that gave that meal its name, that meal really was happy.

IDEA FOR RESPONSE

During the next meal you eat try to be mindful to the entire experience, tasting every bite and being conscious of God providing nutrition for your day.

TAKE TIME TO REFLECT

What are 3 strategies I can employ to live more in the present and be mindful of the needs of those around me?

PRESENT

Just Have Faith

While he was still speaking, people from the synagogue official's house arrived and said, "Your daughter has died; why trouble the teacher any longer?" Disregarding the message that was reported, Jesus said to the synagogue official, "Do not be afraid; just have faith."He did not allow anyone to accompany him inside except Peter, James, and John, the brother of James. When they arrived at the house of the synagogue official, he caught sight of a commotion, people weeping and wailing loudly. So he went in and said to them, "Why this commotion and weeping? The child is not dead but asleep." And they ridiculed him. Then he put them all out. He took along the child's father and mother and those who were with him and entered the room where the child was. He took the child by the hand and said to her, "Talitha koum," which means, "Little girl, I say to you, arise!" The girl, a child of twelve, arose immediately and walked around. [At that] they were utterly astounded.

—Mark 5:35-42

I remember when I was a teenager involved in youth ministry, there was a man in our area that would frequent retreats and lock-in's, telling the story of his daughter who was essentially brain-dead in a hospital bed. She had been given no chance to survive, so he was asked to give the directive to take her off life support. To aid in his discernment process, he went to Mass in the hospital chapel. On his way up the Communion aisle, somehow the Eucharist fell to the floor in front of him. He bent over, picked up the Eucharist, and consumed it. A few people at that Mass had witnessed this occurrence. A man who was there afterwards spoke to him on the way to the elevator. The stranger told him that because Jesus had fallen and he had bent down to pick Him up, a miracle was in store for him. When he got off the elevator for his daughter's floor, he saw that a great commotion had begun and nurses were racing down the hall: to his daughter's room. With anguish, he ran to the room, and this supposedly brain-dead girl, the one he would have to take off life support, sat up and said, "I am hungry." As the years went by, that girl went on to attend Georgetown University and graduate with honors.

I do not remember that man's name. I hope I have not misrepresented details of the story, since the last time I heard it was 30 years ago.

However, the impact of the story has never left me. It taught me the same thing Jesus taught those who witnessed him healing the daughter of Jarius: anything is possible with God. As Everyday Stewards, we are always looking for the small actions that make big differences. God takes what we offer in a simple action and performs miracles. The words of Jesus to Jarius should be in our minds everyday as we go forth into a chaotic world where things are unsure: "Do not be afraid; just have faith."

IDEA FOR RESPONSE
Take a risk and finally reach out to that person you have been afraid to contact for whatever reason. Do not be afraid; just have faith!

TAKE TIME TO REFLECT
What are 3 things in my life that God is calling me to let go of and just have faith?

∽

NO FEAR

Lost and Found

Beloved, if God so loved us, we also must love one another. No one has ever seen God. Yet, if we love one another, God remains in us, and his love is brought to perfection in us. This is how we know that we remain in him and he in us, that he has given us of his Spirit. Moreover, we have seen and testify that the Father sent his Son as savior of the world.

—1 John 4:11-14

When I was around the age of 6, my good friend, Max, moved away. I had known him for less than two years, but I was so fond of him, his moving away really hurt. I was living in Northern Virginia and he was moving to Pittsburgh. Pittsburgh might as well have been in another country. I knew it was far and that was the end of this relationship. I woke up in the middle of the night after he had left that day, crying and yelling. My mother's arms tried to comfort me as well as they could. But this was real pain, even for a 6 year old. It was love.

The First Letter of Saint John states, "Yet, if we love one another, God remains in us, and his love is brought to perfection in us. This is how we know that we remain in him and he is us." I do not want to make too bold a statement or reduce John's words to simple sentiment, but I think the love I felt that night when I was 6 was pretty close to the perfected love mentioned in the passage. A child, so innocent and still untouched by the cynicism and apathy of an adult world, experienced something so deep and hard to understand that I am certain my mother classified it as immature emotions that would quickly fade away. As adults, we think that all the time. Yet 40 years later, I still vividly remember it. I cannot remember Max's last name or visualize his face, but I can still recall the feelings and emotions of that event.

What if we tried harder to take John's words to heart and love more people like a child loves a true friend? John tells us that in that love God is present. That night when I was 6 I may have lost a friend, but I think I found God.

IDEA FOR RESPONSE

Search out an old friend you have not seen for many years and contact the person to see how he or she is doing.

TAKE TIME TO REFLECT

Who are 3 people I need to love more? How can God assist me in becoming more gracious and open to them?

PERFECT LOVE

Healing Our Doubt

Thomas, called Didymus, one of the Twelve, was not with them when Jesus came. So the other disciples said to him, "We have seen the Lord." But he said to them, "Unless I see the mark of the nails in his hands and put my finger into the nailmarks and put my hand into his side, I will not believe." Now a week later his disciples were again inside and Thomas was with them. Jesus came, although the doors were locked, and stood in their midst and said, "Peace be with you." Then he said to Thomas, "Put your finger here and see my hands, and bring your hand and put it into my side, and do not be unbelieving, but believe." Thomas answered and said to him, "My Lord and my God!" Jesus said to him, "Have you come to believe because you have seen me? Blessed are those who have not seen and have believed."

—John 20:24-29

The RCIA experience continues after Easter Vigil during a period of mystagogy. I think that is a big word that means, "Well, Easter Vigil is over. Now what?" Years ago when I was leading RCIA in a parish, I remember breaking open the Gospel reading about doubting Thomas. The other apostles had seen Jesus, but Thomas couldn't believe Jesus was alive unless he saw and touched the resurrected man himself. We were discussing the story when a newly baptized woman spoke up and said, "I think Thomas was pretty weak. If I had been him, I would have believed from the start." I remember how sure she was of herself and her statement. The rest of the group agreed that it is human to doubt and sometimes the only thing that can get us through is the grace of God. Of course, this woman thought we were weak also for even saying that! I talked with her several times after that evening, sometimes cautioning her about being so sure of her statement.

Unfortunately, less than two years later, she left Christianity altogether. She was so sure that she never allowed herself to see her own frailty. She was unprepared for the pitfalls life has in store for all of us. I think the Gospel passage about Thomas is so well known because most of us do not see ourselves in the role of the other apostles. We are like Thomas. That doesn't make us bad, or of little faith. That makes us human. Jesus did not scold Thomas, but instead greeted him and the others with, "Peace be with you."

Jesus brings peace in the face of our fears, our pain, and yes, our doubts. His mercy knows no limits. Instead of getting down about our shortcomings, we should rejoice in the fact that the risen Lord is the remedy for our ailments, and the answer for our unbelief.

IDEA FOR RESPONSE
Think of one doctrine of the Church that you find difficult to understand and spend time researching, reading, and praying about it.

TAKE TIME TO REFLECT
When was a time I doubted the presence of God in my life?

FAITH

Like a Fine Wine

"Hear another parable. There was a landowner who planted a vineyard, put a hedge around it, dug a wine press in it, and built a tower. Then he leased it to tenants and went on a journey. When vintage time drew near, he sent his servants to the tenants to obtain his produce."

—Matthew 21:33-34

Did you know there are over eight thousand wineries in North America? Not every winery has a vineyard, but that's a lot of grapes on vines. Where I live in North Carolina, there are now over 120 wineries and/or vineyards throughout the state. With the decline of tobacco as a major cash crop, those fields have become fertile soil for planting grapes. It would seem the famed "Tobacco Road" might be more aptly named "Wine Way."

Everyone should tour a winery and vineyard at least once. Owners and workers enter into a relationship with the land that is 24/7 and 365 days a year, and it is inspiring to observe. The hard work is worth it, especially when you can produce a fine wine that causes a wine drinker to smile (and pay top dollar)! I just can't imagine doing all that work. I am glad it is easier to enjoy wine by just buying it in a store.

Being good stewards in the vineyard of the Lord isn't that easy either. Much is entrusted to us to care for and cultivate. The expectation is that good fruit will be produced. When the time comes that we are asked for the fruits of our labor, we can react negatively because we have not been the most productive of workers. What we sometimes forget is that, with the help of the One who owns the vineyard, we can produce more good fruit than we can imagine.

I have seen the joy in the eyes of a winemaker who has created an award-winning bottle. Making good wine takes practice, commitment, and a love of the craft. Some barrels of wine produced are not good at all. Mistakes are a part of the process. But perseverance can lead to a wine that is spectacular.

IDEA FOR RESPONSE

Take the time God has given to you and go ahead and complete that task that you have put off for awhile. Thank God for the time to complete the job.

TAKE TIME TO REFLECT

What 3 areas in my life do I need God to
help me with greater perseverance?

GOOD FRUIT

Ignorance Is NOT Bliss

Watch carefully then how you live, not as foolish persons but as wise, making the most of the opportunity, because the days are evil. Therefore, do not continue in ignorance, but try to understand what is the will of the Lord.

—Ephesians 5:15-17

A h, to be 19 again! By the time I was 20, I had already changed my major, met with a vocation director about a possible call to the priesthood, and started dating the girl who would end up becoming my wife. When I was 24, I was married and one year away from completing a master's degree. I wish I could look back and say I knew exactly what I was doing, but that would be a lie. However, what I did have going for me is that I always tried to figure out where the Lord was leading me. The process of discerning His will for my life wasn't easy, and I did feel the need to sometimes explore paths briefly to which He was not calling me. But that was an important part of the journey, waiting for God to speak to each situation in which I found myself.

Now, my oldest son is 19 and he must discern God's will for himself. I fear that he will not be as interested in what God may be saying to him. He may choose to go it alone, and even though I know God will be there somewhere, it will be my son calling the shots.

Saint Paul urges us to not continue in ignorance, but to try to discern the will of God. It is interesting that by making decisions based upon all the data we collected, we remain ignorant if we choose not to listen to God's still voice in our lives. The fact is that our lives our not our own and God has given them to us with a purpose and a plan. We can be instruments of God even if we sometimes say no to His requests, but we can never achieve our full potential without constantly discerning His will for us and responding in maturity. Will our sons and daughters be willing to choose His will over ignorance? Their greatest hope lies in us serving as good examples with our lives.

IDEA FOR RESPONSE

Take one day and begin with spending 5 minutes in prayer attempting to discern God's will for you that day.

TAKE TIME TO REFLECT

What steps can I take to better discern God's will for my life? Do I need to spend more time in prayer? Do I need a spiritual director? Do I need more frequent participation in the sacraments?

DISCERNMENT

Speak, Lord, Your Servant Is Listening

Samuel did not yet recognize the LORD, since the word of the LORD had not yet been revealed to him. The LORD called Samuel again, for the third time. Getting up and going to Eli, he said, "Here I am. You called me." Then Eli understood that the LORD was calling the youth. So he said to Samuel, "Go to sleep, and if you are called, reply, 'Speak, LORD, for your servant is listening.'" When Samuel went to sleep in his place, the LORD came and stood there, calling out as before: Samuel, Samuel! Samuel answered, "Speak, for your servant is listening."

—1 Samuel 3:7-10

Several years ago, a woman came to me who was out of work and unsure of where to turn. After taking a strengths assessment, we explored the many gifts God had given her. She had only done one type of job her entire life up until this point, so she began to learn how she was not defined just by that previous experience. She had so much more to offer. After exploration, I had her take a phonebook and create a list of ten jobs that she thought might require the gifts we had identified. Even if she knew little about the occupation or never saw herself doing that job, she was to create a list to the best of her ability. Even before she finished the list, she stepped forward armed with a renewed vision of herself and found a job. It was something she could not have imagined before our discussions.

Samuel heard a voice and tried to respond. Not knowing who was calling him, his response netted him no gain. It was not until Eli advised him on how to respond that he met up with his destiny as a prophet of God.

No call from God is made in isolation from the community. Others can see in us gifts and talents that sometimes we cannot. Discernment enables disciples to become the best of stewards, allowing for the knowledge where they can grow and become the creation that God intended. Apart from the Body of Christ, not only can we not function as God intended, but we are unsure where we fit in the first place.

The Church needs more Samuels so that the Good News can greater impact our society. To that end, there is at least one Eli for every Samuel. God is calling and it is up to us to respond accordingly.

IDEA FOR RESPONSE
Make a list of the different roles you have in life (parent, child, worker, student, etc.) and reflect on where God is in each of those roles.

TAKE TIME TO REFLECT

Who are 3 people in my life that I trust to help me discern how God is calling me and to what He is calling me?

Little Things, Big Effects

He said, "To what shall we compare the kingdom of God, or what parable can we use for it? It is like a mustard seed that, when it is sown in the ground, is the smallest of all the seeds on the earth. But once it is sown, it springs up and becomes the largest of plants and puts forth large branches, so that the birds of the sky can dwell in its shade." With many such parables he spoke the word to them as they were able to understand it.

—Mark 4:30-33

One summer day, my family and I were in a Dollar Store getting provisions for a weekend getaway. You can always find something you can use at a dollar store. My kids picked up these little cartoon character things they said would turn into big towels when you added water. What! First of all, don't you need a towel to be dry when you are wet? Who wants a towel that only gets big when you first get it wet? Second, this trinket measuring one inch was going to transform itself into a towel one could actually use for their body? I was skeptical. But then again, who says no to something like that when it's only a dollar! Well, everybody knows what happened: it worked! Why they couldn't sell me a normal sized towel I don't know. But of course, my kids wouldn't have wanted me to buy just a normal towel.

What can a little mustard seed really become? When something is small it can deceive people into believing it's power is small as well. But just like in Jesus' parable, that mustard seed, when planted and watered, will become a large plant. Our everyday actions sometimes may seem small, but they can have great power to make a difference, even change lives. There is real transformative power in becoming an everyday steward. Your actions and words, like mustard seeds, get planted in the lives of others, and they grow the kingdom of God. But this we know. We have seen the effects of a loving word or gesture. We have seen how giving small amounts of our time, talent, and treasure can change attitudes, emotions, and the lives of others. Jesus tried to teach us about this in His parables. If you still don't get it, stop by the local dollar store. Examples of small things that make big differences are only a buck!

IDEA FOR RESPONSE

In the next few days, try to say 3 kind things that you would not normally say to people you encounter. Watch how it makes a difference in their demeanor.

TAKE TIME TO REFLECT

Who are 3 people you have encountered in your life that have been Christ to you through their actions or words?
What do you think motivated them?

Be Prayerful

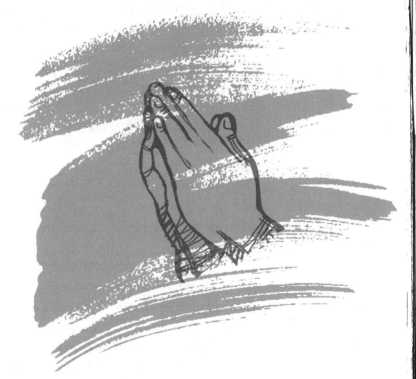

The 2nd Characteristic
of an Everyday Steward

You Are Never Alone

When the time for Pentecost was fulfilled, they were all in one place together. And suddenly there came from the sky a noise like a strong driving wind, and it filled the entire house in which they were. Then there appeared to them tongues as of fire, which parted and came to rest on each one of them. And they were all filled with the holy Spirit and began to speak in different tongues, as the Spirit enabled them to proclaim.

—Acts 2:1-4

My oldest son was having a tougher time than expected in his first year of college. In high school he expected to get As and be one of the smarter kids in the class. Now, he was at a school where everyone came from a similar experience in high school, and he found himself pretty darn average. His mother and I urged him early on to seek some help from a tutor. He gasped. When he was in high school, he WAS the tutor. After some reflection he said, "I just like to do things on my own."

So often many of us are like that. We find it hard to accept help. We think maybe it says something about our lack of capability or skill to reach out for help. When help is offered to us, we can quickly respond, "No thanks, I'm fine." It is amazing how sometimes we are anything but fine.

Living a stewardship way of life as a committed disciple of Jesus is not easy. In fact, we are guaranteed to fail. That inevitable failure is called sin. Grace makes it possible for us to continue on the journey. On that first Pentecost, the first followers of Jesus received the Holy Spirit who would guide them. For over 2000 years, that same Spirit moves in us and guides us. Help for the journey is always available. Sin and temptation constantly seeks to impede our steps. But through the gifts of this Spirit we can discern and make wise judgments, lessening the toll life can exact on us. Reach out and take the hand of God allow His Spirit to lead you and guide you. Don't look back after making the journey harder than it needed to be and say, "I just liked doing things on my own." You are never alone.

IDEA FOR RESPONSE

Ask someone to be your prayer partner and talk with that person once a week to discuss how your prayer lives have been that week.

TAKE TIME TO REFLECT

What 3 Gifts of the Spirit do I need the most in my spiritual life?
(They are fear of the Lord, piety, knowledge, understanding,
counsel, wisdom, and fortitude.☺)

HOLY SPIRIT

For God's Sake, Take a Break

The apostles gathered together with Jesus and reported all they had done and taught. He said to them, "Come away by yourselves to a deserted place and rest a while." People were coming and going in great numbers, and they had no opportunity even to eat. So they went off in the boat by themselves to a deserted place.

—Mark 6:30-32

Being a parent is one of those jobs where you never really get to rest. Even on a vacation, a parent never stops performing the tasks of being a parent: providing, driving, disciplining. That's one reason why so many people desire a vacation after their vacation.

There are some people who never rest from work. They have a cell phone to their ear at home, at a restaurant, and, of course, at a hotel during their vacation. Their jobs might be pretty demanding and hopefully they perform their tasks well for their employer, but they always seem preoccupied.

Jesus tried to have His apostles take a break and rest in Mark 6. They had been so consumed with the crowds and had not even had a chance to eat. So Jesus took them to a deserted place. However, the crowds found them there too, so Jesus continued to teach. It does not say what the apostles did during that time, but I am going to guess it wasn't genuine rest.

Everyone needs a rest. The problem is we fail to understand how important it is to rest. We think rest is void of action. Not only is resting an action in itself, it is sometimes the only time we have to spend with God one-on-one. How can we truly say a relationship with God is important when we never spend time alone with God? Not to take the time to rest in God's presence is poor stewardship of time. Apostles need it. Workers need it. Parents need it. Everyone needs rest. Some say we never rest because we feel we do not have permission to rest and people will see us as lazy. Read Mark 6. Sometimes circumstances make it hard to rest, but you have surely been given permission: from Jesus Himself.

IDEA FOR RESPONSE
In the coming week, take 15 minutes to just sit quietly and try to clear your mind and think of nothing. Just allow yourself to rest in God without using words or thoughts.

TAKE TIME TO REFLECT
What are 3 small things in your life that could be changed in order to make life less hectic, therefore making it easier to focus on God?

RELAX

Trust in the Lord

While they were still speaking about this, he stood in their midst and said to them, "Peace be with you." But they were startled and terrified and thought that they were seeing a ghost. Then he said to them, "Why are you troubled? And why do questions arise in your hearts? Look at my hands and my feet, that it is I myself. Touch me and see, because a ghost does not have flesh and bones as you can see I have." And as he said this, he showed them his hands and his feet.

—Luke 24:36-40

Have you ever participated or witnessed activities that were supposed to instruct you on the topic of trust? Some of these activities feature people falling backward with their eyes closed, sometimes even falling off a chair or table. One variation is when the voice of the person asking for trust trails off into the distance. Secretly other people have crept in and are ready to catch the subjects when they fall backwards, but they are being asked to trust the voice that they know is no longer near them. It is often not easy for the people who are being asked to trust, especially if they have never done this before.

Trusting in God is not always easy either. Sometimes we are scared to give up our freedom. Other times we are consumed by doubt. After Jesus rose from the dead, He appeared a few times to His disciples. One time when He appeared right after some of them had encountered Him on the road to Emmaus, He asked them, "Why are you troubled? And why do questions arise in your hearts?" Even with Him in front of their eyes they had a hard time trusting. They were being asked to trust and believe, but just like those in the trust activities mentioned above, that was easier said than done.

What is keeping you from trusting in God? To live a stewardship way of life, trust in God is necessary. There are times when we will begin to question if we can persevere, or if this way of living is even valid and worthwhile. That is only human. But through the Church, sacred Scripture, and the sacraments, our hearts and minds will be opened to the real crucified and risen Lord. And then, if He asks, we will be able to trust and fall back into His loving arms.

IDEA FOR RESPONSE

Search for videos of trust-building activities on YouTube and watch a couple. Try to determine how each activity speaks to your relationship with God.

TAKE TIME TO REFLECT

What are 3 areas of my life where I need to trust in God more fully?

TRUST

Everyday Miracles

On leaving the synagogue he entered the house of Simon and Andrew with James and John. Simon's mother-in-law lay sick with a fever. They immediately told him about her. He approached, grasped her hand, and helped her up. Then the fever left her and she waited on them. When it was evening, after sunset, they brought to him all who were ill or possessed by demons. The whole town was gathered at the door. He cured many who were sick with various diseases, and he drove out many demons, not permitting them to speak because they knew him.

—Mark 1:29-34

Jesus performed miracles of healing quite often in the Gospels. He healed disease, gave sight to the blind, made the lame walk, exorcised demons, and even raised the dead. We believe that He did these things not just because He loved those people, but so those who witnessed such actions or heard the testimonies would believe in Him.

It is a bitter pill to swallow when we pray for healing and it doesn't happen. We can begin to wonder if we prayed hard enough or with enough sincerity. In our pain we can even begin to wonder if God was listening.

But if you think of all this logically, if Jesus healed everyone who asked and everyone He loved, no one would ever be sick or even die. Certainly, He does not love those He heals more than others. And surely miracles do not only happen due to the prayers of professionals.

The wonder of miracles occurs so that we might be reminded that God is still near, and regardless of how it might seem, there is little that separates the natural from the supernatural, and the reality we live in and the one we are moving toward. Everyday stewards can see the presence of God in so many people, places, and situations on a daily basis. The realities of the now and not yet are blended so seamlessly that the definition of a miracle becomes unclear. If a miracle means something extraordinary so that the world may believe, then Jesus really does perform them for all of us. We just have to pay attention.

IDEA FOR RESPONSE
Find someone who needs the everyday miracle of a friend and invite him or her to lunch.

TAKE TIME TO REFLECT
What are 3 things in my life that could be considered small miracles? Have I thanked God for these?

I Am Not God

Then they came to Capernaum, and on the sabbath he entered the synagogue and taught. The people were astonished at his teaching, for he taught them as one having authority and not as the scribes. In their synagogue was a man with an unclean spirit; he cried out, "What have you to do with us, Jesus of Nazareth? Have you come to destroy us? I know who you are—the Holy One of God!" Jesus rebuked him and said, "Quiet! Come out of him!" The unclean spirit convulsed him and with a loud cry came out of him. All were amazed and asked one another, "What is this? A new teaching with authority. He commands even the unclean spirits and they obey him."

—Mark 1:21-27

While at a conference for pastors, I heard someone address the audience with, "Do not think your job is to go about changing the world. Your job is to go about testifying to the truth that the world is already changed through the death and resurrection of Jesus Christ." I was stunned to hear what I already knew: God is God, and I am not. All the work that I do amounts to very little in the face of what God has done. And yet, my little actions can have such a big impact when it is God working through me.

Jesus stunned crowds with His authoritative teaching and His miracles. They were amazed saying, "He commands even the unclean spirits and they obey him." It seemed that He was in control of everything. Of course, He was.

Often times we fall into a trap of thinking that we are the key to success in the actions of social justice, peacemaking, and community building. We think the walls will fall down if we are called away to journey elsewhere. We have succumbed to the lie that it is all due to us, and that God played only a minor role. We forget that God is bigger than that and His plan is always better than ours.

A good steward allows Jesus Christ to exercise His authority in our lives. We give of ourselves freely and work to grow the gifts that have been entrusted to us, but we also submit to His will as to how those gifts will impact the world around us. We do all this knowing that His plan has a beginning and an end. The end has already been determined. We are working in the between times to make the journey reflect more fully the reality of His love.

IDEA FOR RESPONSE
The next time you feel frustration about a situation you cannot control, pray to God these words: "You are God and I am not. Please come to my aid. Amen."

TAKE TIME TO REFLECT

What are 3 aspects of my life I try to control but know I am unable to do so? How can God take control of those situations?

God's Gift of Leisure

Remember the sabbath day—keep it holy. Six days you may labor and do all your work, but the seventh day is a sabbath of the LORD your God. You shall not do any work, either you, your son or your daughter, your male or female slave, your work animal, or the resident alien within your gates. For in six days the LORD made the heavens and the earth, the sea and all that is in them; but on the seventh day he rested. That is why the LORD has blessed the sabbath day and made it holy.

—Exodus 20:8-11

When the summer months come they bring with them increased opportunities for relaxation and recreation. However, our fast moving world would often seek to deny us those gifts of time and space. We can find ourselves in a place where the desire for leisure is seen as a sign of laziness or lack of commitment. But was it not God who gave to us the model of rest by refraining from activity on the seventh day of creation? And if all we have comes from God, by not taking the time for leisure do we not disregard this essential gift?

When we take time to include "inactivity" into our daily life and into our year, we acknowledge that we are not the sum of our career, job, schoolwork, or even parenting. We have been given more by God and sometimes the only way to experience the richness of those gifts is to take a break from that which we normally do. The German Catholic philosopher, Josef Pieper, spent much of his time writing about these very issues. In his book, *Leisure: The Basis of Culture*, he wrote about the dangers of becoming consumed by work. He wrote, *"Of course the world of work begins to become - threatens to become - our only world, to the exclusion of all else. The demands of the working world grow ever more total, grasping ever more completely the whole of human existence."*

Whether it is during summer or another time of the year, let us be good stewards by taking time to rest in the Lord. At times the fields must lie fallow to be watered by the rain and nourished by the sun. This will provide time to the sower to decide the best crops to plant and seeds to sow. Then his harvest, when it arrives, will be that much fuller.

IDEA FOR RESPONSE
Take a day off from work or a Saturday and give yourself permission to do nothing. Take time to rest in God.

TAKE TIME TO REFLECT
When were the 3 best occurrences of real relaxation for me?
Did I consciously invite God into those times?

LEISURE

Calculating Love

When the Pharisees heard that he had silenced the Sadducees, they gathered together, and one of them [a scholar of the law] tested him by asking, "Teacher, which commandment in the law is the greatest?" He said to him, "You shall love the Lord, your God, with all your heart, with all your soul, and with all your mind. This is the greatest and the first commandment. The second is like it: You shall love your neighbor as yourself. The whole law and the prophets depend on these two commandments."

—Matthew 22:34-40

Have you ever Googled the word "love"? If you did you may have come across something called the Love Calculator. It is a website where you can supply two names, and the percentage chance of a successful relationship is calculated. Curious, I entered my name and my wife's. Twenty percent! I hope my wife doesn't read this!

I then decided to add my name and God. A whopping thirteen percent! Then for the last attempt, I put in my name and Jesus. A very disappointing zero percent! Am I that unlovable? Of course, then I read the small print at the bottom of the page: "Please note that this site has no serious intention whatsoever." Shocking!

The truth is, the modern world increasingly seems to have no real idea what love is or how to determine when love is real. That makes the seemingly simple words of Jesus about loving God and your neighbor very complex indeed. How can you love God with your all your heart, soul, and mind when you have no idea what the act of loving means? And then, what constitutes loving a neighbor? To make it more complicated, Jesus commands you to love them like you love yourself. I bet you can agree with me that there are a lot of people out there who do not even come close to loving themselves. Knowing what love is in modern times is just not that easy. How is a well-meaning person able to find out the true meaning of love?

You don't know what true love is? I think you do. Turn your eyes to that crucifix hanging in your church, home, or office. The answer was given over two thousand years ago, and the image remains for the entire world to see.

IDEA FOR RESPONSE
Find a piece of paper or note card and a pen and sit down to write a note to someone.about how much you love that person.

TAKE TIME TO REFLECT

How has my understanding of love changed over my life? When I look at a crucifix, what does it say to me about the nature of love?

SACRIFICE

Be Grateful

The 3rd Characteristic
of an Everyday Steward

The Real McCoy

Set me as a seal upon your heart,
as a seal upon your arm;
For Love is strong as Death,
longing is fierce as Sheol.
Its arrows are arrows of fire,
flames of the divine.
Deep waters cannot quench love,
nor rivers sweep it away.

—Song of Songs 8:6-7a

I collect smiley faces. The crown jewels of my collection are Harvey Ball autographed smileys and McCoy pottery smileys. When I started my collection, I looked for the McCoy symbol on each pottery piece, to verify it was a "real McCoy." The stamp of the symbol told me that it had been made in the 1970s and was indeed made by the Ohio manufacturer. Without a stamp, I could only assume it was a counterfeit or copycat piece, coming from nowhere special and belonging to no known entity.

In a 2009 address, Pope Emeritus Benedict XVI spoke about the Holy Trinity in this way: "The name of the Blessed Trinity is, in a certain sense, imprinted upon all things because all that exists, down to the last particle, is in relation; in this way we catch a glimpse of God as relationship and ultimately, Creator Love. All things derive from love, aspire to love and move impelled by love." That means that you and I, and all material things, bear this imprint. The mark indicates our origin and Creator.

This implies three important realities: 1) All creation is important and precious; 2) All creation belongs to the Creator whose mark is imprinted on it; and, 3) The origin and purpose of that creation is love. A good steward then should cherish everything and everyone around them, and treat all of it with great care and compassion. Even our belongings and resources used to co-create with God all bear His mark. Our children, parents, siblings, friends, neighbors, and enemies, all bear the mark. There is nothing or no one who belongs to an unknown entity. It is all God's. It is all the real McCoy.

IDEA FOR RESPONSE

Take a piece of paper and list as many people and things you can think of that you love. Fold it up and keep it at the back of this book for future reference.

TAKE TIME TO REFLECT

What is something or who is someone I treat with less respect than deserved?

Lessons from the Playground

"It was not you who chose me, but I who chose you and appointed you to go and bear fruit that will remain, so that whatever you ask the Father in my name he may give you."

—John 15:16

Do you remember being a child and deciding on captains to choose sides for a game of kickball, soccer, or other sport requiring little more than a ball? Kids sat on a curb, waiting to hear their fate. "Surely, I will not be picked last," each boy or girl thought. But alas, someone always had to be last. The worst part was it often came down to one kid who thought he was not too horrible, and one kid who knew he was horrible. Guess who was picked first, assuring that the sole survivor of this ritual was left to question why he or she even left the house that day? Good times!

Most of the time, to be chosen can make a person feel wanted or needed. You realize that someone else sees something in you that they respect and value. You become a part of something bigger than yourself, a community, even if it is a community of two, such as in a marriage.

Most people would probably say they chose Christ. Even a popular song's refrain exclaims, "I will choose Christ." However, what you have chosen is an action. If you are Christian, you choose to follow, imitate, and even become Christ. But you did not choose Christ. He chose YOU.

Jesus speaks in John's Gospel to His disciples, "It was not you who chose me, but I who chose you." Do not think for a second that it was your choosing to get into this game. You were the one chosen. And there was no first, middle, or last. Someone saw something in you of great value and He made sure to choose you. And no matter how many times you mess up and start to feel like you are not good enough for Him, He reminds you that you are still a star on His team. He would choose you all over again.

IDEA FOR RESPONSE

Go out and treat yourself to something delicious that you love.
Celebrate the fact that you have been chosen by God.

TAKE TIME TO REFLECT

*Since I am chosen and have great value, what 3 talents or gifts do
I have that I can give back to God with a grateful heart?*

CHOSEN

Nourishment for the Job Ahead

"I am the true vine, and my Father is the vine grower. He takes away every branch in me that does not bear fruit, and everyone that does he prunes so that it bears more fruit. You are already pruned because of the word that I spoke to you. Remain in me, as I remain in you. Just as a branch cannot bear fruit on its own unless it remains on the vine, so neither can you unless you remain in me. I am the vine, you are the branches. Whoever remains in me and I in him will bear much fruit, because without me you can do nothing. Anyone who does not remain in me will be thrown out like a branch and wither; people will gather them and throw them into a fire and they will be burned. If you remain in me and my words remain in you, ask for whatever you want and it will be done for you."

—John 15:1-7

I remember one woman I had the privilege of working with in RCIA, who ultimately decided to become Catholic because of the Eucharist. She had experiences in other denominations that held celebrations of holy Communion, but they did not see the Eucharist as the real presence of Jesus Christ. When she realized what the bread and wine truly became in the Mass, she stated that she could not truly be who she wanted and needed to be without weekly participation in Mass and reception of Eucharist. After she became Catholic, she soon became a daily communicant for this very same reason.

In *The Life of a Christian Steward: A Reflection on the Logic of Commitment*, published by the International Catholic Stewardship Council, one reads, "To be most effective in service to God and humankind, Christian stewardship must stem from the liturgical worship in the Church. Here one finds the supernatural motive, the word of faith, and the grace necessary to get the job done." Then the document quotes John 15, with Jesus teaching, "I am the vine, and you are the branches." The reality is that without nourishment from the vine, Jesus, the branches, you and I, cannot bear fruit and will wither and die.

Recommit yourself to the Eucharist. Come to church in time to calm your heart and mind. Be attentive and participate. Be mindful of your actions, your senses, and your intentions. Approach the Eucharist reflecting on the reality that you are encountering and consuming the actual risen Lord. Do not let moments in Mass pass you by without reflection. Then, you will find the nourishment needed to bring the Good News of Easter to the world. You will be equipped to "get the job done."

IDEA FOR RESPONSE
Take a tour of a local winery or vineyard and listen to how wine is made. Take note of the value of good vines in producing good grapes.

TAKE TIME TO REFLECT

What are the 3 aspects of a Sunday Mass that really speak to me as I try to more closely follow Jesus Christ?

Thanks for Everything

For everything created by God is good, and nothing is to be rejected when received with thanksgiving, for it is made holy by the invocation of God in prayer.

—1 Timothy 4:4-5

I was sitting in my car, waiting to pick up my daughter from an area teen Bible study. When I finally saw her I noticed she was walking with her friend from school, who had recently been talking about getting baptized. Her parents were divorced and because of circumstances beyond her control, she never received the sacrament. Now she was older and growing in faith and longed to belong. I realized both she and my daughter were coming toward my car. I rolled down the window. My daughter's friend just wanted to say hello and thank me for inviting and taking her to Mass with us the previous Sunday. I told her she was welcome anytime. I thought to myself how nice it was for her to thank me for something I had not even thought much about.

When you begin to see all that is around you as gift, you cannot help but give thanks. You give thanks for the obvious: life, family, and love. But you also give thanks for the smaller things: a ride, a gesture, and a prayer. And you begin to realize that all actions of thanks, whether it is directly to God in prayer, or it is to a person who has been kind, end up glorifying God. For it was God that created all things and any acknowledgement of that goodness glorifies the Creator.

Everyday stewards can find it easier to be optimistic in this crazy world because they see life as so precious and all that works in concert to sustain it as good. The gratitude expressed and experienced by a person provides a pathway to hope when it all seems hopeless, and to love in the face of hate. It makes things like the longing of a young girl to be washed clean in baptismal waters possible in the face of a culture, and perhaps parents, that see this as foolish. Thanks be to God.

IDEA FOR RESPONSE

Sit down and handwrite a thank-you note to someone that deserves your gratitude. Make sure you send it. (Yes, snail mail!)

TAKE TIME TO REFLECT

How can I begin to show greater gratitude for those who have really touched my life?

GRATITUDE

Leading Them to Love

And people brought to him a deaf man who had a speech impediment and begged him to lay his hand on him. He took him off by himself away from the crowd. He put his finger into the man's ears and, spitting, touched his tongue; then he looked up to heaven and groaned, and said to him, "Ephphatha!" (that is, "Be opened!") And [immediately] the man's ears were opened, his speech impediment was removed, and he spoke plainly. He ordered them not to tell anyone. But the more he ordered them not to, the more they proclaimed it.

—Mark 7:32-36

I remember being a child when just the invasion of a frightening thought could send me running into my parents' bed for safety. One night it is was the movie I watched on television before I went to bed. Another night it was the sudden thought of what if someone I loved suddenly died. Whatever the reason for fear, the closeness of my mother or father could easily make all things better. I felt completely secure.

As I got older, I began to realize that my parents couldn't protect me from everything. That was okay because most of what I feared as a child now seemed, well, childish. Later in my life, my own children would seek the comfortable confines of their parents' bed, and I would remember those youthful days once again.

I cannot, just like my parents before me, offer much to calm the fears of my children other than give them love. However, I can lead them to the One who has the power to truly defeat anything or anyone that seeks to harm them. He can help them see when they are blind, teach them to speak when they are speechless, and help them walk again after they have fallen. Of course, His name is Jesus.

I wish I could do all those things for them, because my love is so overwhelming for them. But my job is to lead them to the One who can do all these things. He has entrusted them to me and I am called to return them to Him. That's what a good steward would do. When they are young, they can easily feel like my love is enough. But when they are older, they will need the One whose love is truly enough, because it is not merely human, it is miraculous.

IDEA FOR RESPONSE
Think of someone who is living in fear or someone who has a fear of something specific. Pray for that person and then reach out to him or her.

TAKE TIME TO REFLECT
Who is someone God has entrusted to me to lead him or her closer to Him?

JESUS

Be Gracious

The 4th Characteristic
of an Everyday Steward

Tummies Full of Love

When Jesus raised his eyes and saw that a large crowd was coming to him, he said to Philip, "Where can we buy enough food for them to eat?" He said this to test him, because he himself knew what he was going to do. Philip answered him, "Two hundred days' wages worth of food would not be enough for each of them to have a little [bit]." One of his disciples, Andrew, the brother of Simon Peter, said to him, "There is a boy here who has five barley loaves and two fish; but what good are these for so many?" Jesus said, "Have the people recline." Now there was a great deal of grass in that place. So the men reclined, about five thousand in number. Then Jesus took the loaves, gave thanks, and distributed them to those who were reclining, and also as much of the fish as they wanted. When they had had their fill, he said to his disciples, "Gather the fragments left over, so that nothing will be wasted." So they collected them, and filled twelve wicker baskets with fragments from the five barley loaves that had been more than they could eat. When the people saw the sign he had done, they said, "This is truly the Prophet, the one who is to come into the world."

—John 6:5-14

For many years Alberta Hairston was the Catholic campus minister at North Carolina A&T University and Bennett College, both traditionally black institutions. She operated out of a house named for Sr. Thea Bowman, a great African-American sister and evangelist who helped found the Black Catholic Sisters Conference. It was a small house on one of the campuses, but was open to all students, Catholic or non-Catholic. When Momma H, as she was called, started in the ministry, she had no advanced degree but she had experience helping the campus minister before her. Also, she had a great love of the Lord and His people. She also had a tremendously powerful tool of evangelization: the kitchen.

Alberta knew that if she could have a chance to feed their bellies, she could then begin to feed their souls. Of course, she could never be certain how many students might show up at a meal. But that did not matter, because somehow there was always enough. Did she perform miracles, like Jesus feeding the 5000? Well, a tray of cornbread never instantly became 3 trays of cornbread! But she did have one of the same key characteristics as Jesus: love. You see, there was always enough food for everyone because Momma H wasn't feeding college students just cornbread, chicken, and mac and cheese; she was feeding them with love.

Love changes everything. It can lead to lost souls feeling like they belong. It can help a blind person see the truth. Love is the root of true hospitality, and both Jesus and Momma H have that. There are people all throughout our lives that feel like there is not enough in this life for them. But with our actions of love, they miraculously are filled with what they need. Of course, a tray of good cornbread doesn't hurt either.

IDEA FOR RESPONSE
Identify someone who has been going through a difficult time and bring that person dinner or take him or her out to eat.

TAKE TIME TO REFLECT
What are 3 everyday actions that I perform that show people I love them?

HOSPITALITY

A Living Witness

He summoned the Twelve and began to send them out two by two and gave them authority over unclean spirits. He instructed them to take nothing for the journey but a walking stick—no food, no sack, no money in their belts. They were, however, to wear sandals but not a second tunic. He said to them, "Wherever you enter a house, stay there until you leave from there. Whatever place does not welcome you or listen to you, leave there and shake the dust off your feet in testimony against them." So they went off and preached repentance.

—Mark 6:7-12

When one works for a parish, church organization, or is closely aligned with a Christian community, it causes some to be nervous. I always get a kick out of meeting people for the first time and when they hear I work in the Church, they want to tell me how they have been meaning to get back to attending a church, or how they have not yet found a place to attend on Sundays since they moved to the area... like 10 years ago. Of course, it's funny now how all my non-Catholic friends want to tell me how much they like Pope Francis, as if I have tea with him every Friday at the Vatican.

That being said, as a Christian I do have a responsibility to share the Good News with others. If I had a powerful experience losing weight, finding a great restaurant, or hearing a great piece of music, I would want to share that with others. Surely my relationship with Jesus Christ and what He has done for me by transforming my life is better than any weight loss, steak, or new band. How can I hide the most important aspect of my life?

Being a good steward helps them see what Jesus has done for me. They see that I am striving to be more giving, more gracious, and more welcoming. Hopefully, they see something they want also. I can tell them more about my faith, but hopefully my actions will cause them to inquire first. If they choose to reject me for who I am I can only pray the next good steward that crosses their path intrigues them more. Meanwhile, I can love them as they are, people just like me, looking for what I have already found.

IDEA FOR RESPONSE
Write one social media post online (Facebook, Twitter, etc.) about what God has meant to you in your life.

TAKE TIME TO REFLECT
Who are 3 people I know who need to grow in knowledge and love of Jesus Christ?

SHARE

The Last Shall Be First

They came to Capernaum and, once inside the house, he began to ask them, "What were you arguing about on the way?" But they remained silent. They had been discussing among themselves on the way who was the greatest. Then he sat down, called the Twelve, and said to them, "If anyone wishes to be first, he shall be the last of all and the servant of all."

—Mark 9:33-35

I no longer participate in the Black Friday rituals of waiting for stores to open at 5 or 6 in the morning, just so I can get the deal of a lifetime. When I was younger, that held a certain fascination for me, but today sleep is my best friend and maddening crowds are just that: maddening. Besides, the times my wife or I ever got a deal that amazing were few. Most of the time you struggled to be the first in line so you could find great treasure, only to walk away with more stuff to put in the garage next to last year's stuff. You paid less for the stuff than normal, but in the end, it wasn't worth a whole lot anyway.

It seems to be human nature to want to be first, the best, or the greatest. We think there is a great value to be on top. We are sure if we can be better than everyone else, the prize waiting for us will ultimately satisfy. Jesus' disciples argued about which one of them was the greatest. Jesus explained to them that the greatest was the one who chose to be last by serving all. The prize apparently awaits us after we have allowed all others to step ahead of us. We must be completely humbled in order to rise up victorious.

Good stewardship is about giving all we have so that others might not want for anything. This is truly being gracious and offering hospitality to all we encounter. Throughout our lives there are so many people to whom we have the chance to offer our time, talent, and treasure. This is where the real reward lies: in the love of others and God. Besides, we always have heard it is better to give than receive. How great was it to get that DVD player I didn't need that sits in my garage anyway?

IDEA FOR RESPONSE

The next time you are in a store checkout line, allow the person behind you to go ahead of you.

TAKE TIME TO REFLECT

What is an area in my life where I let pride get the best of me?
How can I learn to be satisfied not being first or the best?

SERVE OTHERS

We Are Never Alone

After six days Jesus took Peter, James, and John and led them up a high mountain apart by themselves. And he was transfigured before them, and his clothes became dazzling white, such as no fuller on earth could bleach them. Then Elijah appeared to them along with Moses, and they were conversing with Jesus. Then Peter said to Jesus in reply, "Rabbi, it is good that we are here! Let us make three tents: one for you, one for Moses, and one for Elijah." He hardly knew what to say, they were so terrified. Then a cloud came, casting a shadow over them; then from the cloud came a voice, "This is my beloved Son. Listen to him." Suddenly, looking around, they no longer saw anyone but Jesus alone with them.

—Mark 9:2-8

Family is important to me. I never experienced a large family growing up. I loved marrying into a larger family that all got together for certain holidays of the year. And now that I have three children, I would guess we sit down for dinner at the dining table more than most modern families. The world is a very vast space with many challenges, but our little carved out corner of it is always a place of faith, hope, and love.

As a good steward, not only am I called to cherish the gift of my family and work hard so those in it may flourish, I am also called to see them in the context of my larger family of faith. There are times we must come together as a smaller family unit, but we also must participate fully in our larger family, both in our parish and in our global Church. Our identity comes from both community experiences.

When the apostles saw Elijah and Moses transfigured before them, they saw patriarchs of their family of faith, in other words, family. Like gracious stewards that know the importance of hospitality, they immediately wanted to prepare shelter for them. Their identity in this new family of apostles was given a more profound meaning by their experience of the larger family of faith.

We never stand alone in this world. Even if we have no one left in our immediate bloodline, there is a family that calls to us for engagement. During the seasons of Advent and Lent, our families of faith are gathering more frequently and inviting us inside. The more we participate in our family events, the more grounded we become. The more we share with our family, the more we are sure of our identity. We belong.

IDEA FOR RESPONSE
Be sure to attend the next parish social event, but this time, be sure to invite someone not from your parish to go with you.

TAKE TIME TO REFLECT

Who are 3 people who can count on me to be there for them no matter the reason?

COMMUNITY

Gold, Frankincense, Paper

And behold, the star that they had seen at its rising preceded them, until it came and stopped over the place where the child was. They were overjoyed at seeing the star, and on entering the house they saw the child with Mary his mother. They prostrated themselves and did him homage. Then they opened their treasures and offered him gifts of gold, frankincense, and myrrh.

—Matthew 2:9b-11

I remember in 3rd grade I sang "The Little Drummer Boy" in the parish school Christmas program. I walked in pretending to play a cardboard drum and sang about how I had nothing else to give the newborn King except my drum playing. Three other students got to portray the Wise Men and give to Jesus gold, frankincense, and myrrh. Of course, at the age of 8 I couldn't even play the drum, so needless to say my gift seemed pretty shabby compared to the ones given by the 3 with deep pockets.

What can God do with such a small gift as the song of a little boy? The reality is that our gifts do not increase the goodness of God. He does not need my song, or my gold. I don't need the art of my children from school. I don't need to watch my son play soccer, or dance with my daughter at the daddy/daughter dance. I want to, and they need me to. I am excited and filled with joy to participate in the lives of my children. And they need to feel my love and know they rest in my heart.

The baby Jesus did not need the riches of the Wise Men, or the drumming of a little boy. He wanted them. He still wants them. He is filled with great joy at the offerings of God's children. And that little boy needed to offer to his King the only thing he possessed. He needed to feel His love and know that he belonged to Him. On this celebration of the Epiphany of the Lord, what will you offer to Jesus? Whatever it is, I am sure He will love it, even if all you have is something like a silly old paper drum.

IDEA FOR RESPONSE

Make or buy a very inexpensive gift, wrap it nicely, and give it to someone you love.

TAKE TIME TO REFLECT

What 3 simple gifts does God want from me that I have hesitated giving because I worry they are insignificant?

SIMPLE GIFTS

There Is Much to Be Done

"Then the king will say to those on his right, 'Come, you who are blessed by my Father. Inherit the kingdom prepared for you from the foundation of the world. For I was hungry and you gave me food, I was thirsty and you gave me drink, a stranger and you welcomed me, naked and you clothed me, ill and you cared for me, in prison and you visited me.' Then the righteous will answer him and say, 'Lord, when did we see you hungry and feed you, or thirsty and give you drink? When did we see you a stranger and welcome you, or naked and clothe you? When did we see you ill or in prison, and visit you?' And the king will say to them in reply, 'Amen, I say to you, whatever you did for one of these least brothers of mine, you did for me.'"

—Matthew 25:34-40

Growing up Catholic means I must have heard a million times the passage in Matthew's Gospel about how doing things for the "least of these" means you have done them for Jesus. Okay, that is an exaggeration to make a point. But it has been a slogan for so many social justice activities, from clothing and canned food drives, to letter writing campaigns and peaceful protests.

Growing up I only knew how to help the least of these through the school and church activities of the time. Today, YouTube and GodTube are filled with videos of creative ways people reach out to one another. Have you seen the one about the pizza party for the homeless? How about the fake lottery ticket or the house bought from online donations for a poor man? There are even videos of people paying for the car behind them at the drive-through! The awesome thing about this is that it serves as a witness to others. It is not boasting but instead sharing the Good News. Giving and good stewardship can be contagious!

Our pastor has several times over the years handed out $10 bills to confirmation candidates and asked them to "pay it forward." They can keep the money or use it to make a difference in someone else's life. One teen planted a garden for an elderly woman. One bought ingredients for brownies and sold them to give even more than $10 to charity. The teens not only learned something about good stewardship in the process, but also served as great examples to the parish community.

As always, there is much to be done. The King is coming soon! Let's spread the news and some love at the same time!

IDEA FOR RESPONSE
Today, find a way to do something for someone you do not know, or at least do not know well, and then ask the person to "pay it forward."

TAKE TIME TO REFLECT

In what ways do I regularly care for "the least of these?" What can I change in my life to make this part of it more profound?

OUTREACH

Cherished Treasures

For we are God's co-workers; you are God's field, God's building. According to the grace of God given to me, like a wise master builder I laid a foundation, and another is building upon it. But each one must be careful how he builds upon it, for no one can lay a foundation other than the one that is there, namely, Jesus Christ.

—1 Corinthians 3:9-11

Catholics who attend daily Mass come across interesting feasts all the time: unknown saints and martyrs, various titles for Jesus and Our Lady, the Chair of St. Peter. One of the most interesting feasts you might encounter is the Dedication of the Lateran Basilica each November. Many probably ask, "A feast for the dedication of a building?" This is not just any building. It is the first church built after the legalization of Christianity by Constantine in the fourth century. It some ways, it held the font through which a baptismal revolution changed the world.

Good stewards cherish that which has been handed down to them through the ages. My pastor once likened stewardship to being in an antique store. When you purchase an antique you take responsibility not only for that material possession, but for all the memories of lives it has touched through the generations. You can almost feel the presence of the one who made the item, as well as those who possessed it and used it before you. Now it is yours to care for and, if it is truly of value, you will probably pass it on years later to the next steward.

What we create with God and what we take care of in this material world helps provide meaning in our lives. The picture your child, who is now an adult, drew when he was 5 rests comfortably in your hope chest. The book given to you by a friend on your birthday stands at attention on the bookshelf. The souvenir you bought on that once-in-a-lifetime trip reminds you of that special time as you sit daily at your desk. Yes, it is true, all these material things, just like the Lateran Basilica, will some day pass away when Christ returns. But what these things represent will live on forever.

As good stewards, we see the value of what is unseen as well as that which is seen. Take good care of all those things entrusted to you. They are important tools on the journey, to remind us what is important and where we are going.

IDEA FOR RESPONSE
Find something you have possession of that means something to you. Perhaps it reminds you of a person, a place, or an important time in your life. Spend 5 minutes reflecting on why it means something to you and what part it plays in your life.

TAKE TIME TO REFLECT

What is 1 thing I have that I can pass on to someone else that will be meaningful? Can I pass it on now while I am still alive and able to share in the joy of that exchange?

PASS IT ON

The Heart of Hospitality

"Then he said to his servants, 'The feast is ready, but those who were invited were not worthy to come. Go out, therefore, into the main roads and invite to the feast whomever you find.' The servants went out into the streets and gathered all they found, bad and good alike, and the hall was filled with guests."

—Matthew 22:8-10

To be invited to dinner is a form of hospitality as old as the human race. Sitting around a table, eating and drinking, is a way to share our lives with each other and show that we care. When we are shown hospitality, we always become more receptive to others because they have shared a part of themselves.

Hospitality is a component of stewardship that can never be trivialized. How we treat people is important not only when it comes to larger affairs, such as helping those in need, comforting the distraught, or doing a favor for someone, but also in our everyday interactions. If every breath we take belongs to God, then at every turn our interactions with people have the potential of bringing someone closer to the source of that breath.

This reality hit me the other day in the grocery store. I was in the checkout line with a cart full of items. While waiting, a woman came up behind me with two bags of chicken tenders and a baby in her arms. I offered to let her cut in front of me. She was so grateful but equally surprised someone would offer that to her. My simple action that day didn't lead to a full-blown evangelizing event. But it could have and sometimes it does.

Everyday stewardship means that when we see all aspects of our life as gifts from God, then in the ordinary we see opportunities for the extraordinary. In a grocery checkout line, on the bus, and walking across a college campus, we find chances to do something extraordinary. We have a chance to raise the mundane to a level where God can be noticed. In this reality, the heart of real hospitality is found.

IDEA FOR RESPONSE

The next time you are shopping look for at least 3 opportunities to offer hospitality with a kind action or word.

TAKE TIME TO REFLECT

Who are 3 people to whom I can offer greater hospitality in my life? How can God help me change?

EXTRAORDINARY

Be Committed

The 5th Characteristic
of an Everyday Steward

Better than Elvis

He answered them, "It is not for you to know the times or seasons that the Father has established by his own authority. But you will receive power when the Holy Spirit comes upon you, and you will be my witnesses in Jerusalem, throughout Judea and Samaria, and to the ends of the earth." When he had said this, as they were looking on, he was lifted up, and a cloud took him from their sight. While they were looking intently at the sky as he was going, suddenly two men dressed in white garments stood beside them. They said, "Men of Galilee, why are you standing there looking at the sky? This Jesus who has been taken up from you into heaven will return in the same way as you have seen him going into heaven."

—Acts 1:7-11

There is a great need in our current world for more Jesus sightings. You used to hear about Elvis sightings from time to time, but we do not need sightings of the King of Rock n Roll. We need sightings of the King of Kings.

Of course, when we celebrate the feast of His ascension into heaven, we also reflect on the fact that in bodily form He no longer walks the earth, and we await His second coming. Some see His image on trees, buildings, and even toast. I am not sure that would be a very helpful plan, even if God really had dreamt that up as a way to remind us of Him. But God's real plan did include a way for Jesus to continually be seen in the world. That plan involved us.

The scriptural account of Jesus' ascension contains clear instructions on what we are to do until He returns. Those instructions entail proclaiming the Gospel, baptizing those who believe, and healing the sick. As a poem attributed to Teresa of Avila points out, "Christ has no body now on earth but yours." The poem speaks about our hands, feet, eyes, and body being those of Christ. When we move in the world, we not only bear the name of Christian, we have become Christ. As intentional disciples and good stewards, we realize that our role in this Divine plan is of utmost importance. Jesus is present to the world through us. So, go forth everyday from your home, ready to bring Christ to every person you meet. And then, just maybe, more people will say, "I think I saw Jesus today." That would be better than an infinite number of Elvis sightings.

IDEA FOR RESPONSE
Commit to telling a different person something about your faith life for 3 days in a row. It doesn't have to be overly profound; just share about yourself.

TAKE TIME TO REFLECT
What are 3 things that keep me from becoming a more committed follower of Jesus?

THE CHRIST

Lead Us Not into Temptation

"If your hand causes you to sin, cut it off. It is better for you to enter into life maimed than with two hands to go into Gehenna, into the unquenchable fire. And if your foot causes you to sin, cut it off. It is better for you to enter into life crippled than with two feet to be thrown into Gehenna. And if your eye causes you to sin, pluck it out. Better for you to enter into the kingdom of God with one eye than with two eyes to be thrown into Gehenna, where 'their worm does not die, and the fire is not quenched.'"

—Mark 9:43-48

You can't guess how many times the phrase has been heard in my family, "It's time to start eating healthy." You can't guess because I can't even guess, and it's my family! When that intense awareness arrives that we have as a collective unit all fallen too far off the bandwagon, we begin to devise a plan. Exercise, more water, lower carbs, more water, leafy greens, and more water: You get the picture. Also, every time we must remove all bad foods from the house and make a commitment never to buy such items again. These delicious snacks will lead us down the path to ruin. They must be eliminated.

Of course, no cookie ever made me eat it. But I have chosen to eat many cookies. My will at times is just too weak to resist eating it. So, it actually is a good move not to have it in the pantry. There is no reason to unnecessarily tempt oneself.

In Mark's Gospel, Jesus goes to extremes to make this very point. He suggests that even if a body part causes us to sin, cut it off. Of course, my hand, eye, or foot has never forced me to do anything. However, the point is well taken that we cannot allow ourselves to fall back into the same patterns of sin, again and again.

When applying this theme to stewardship, we cannot allow ourselves to come up against the same obstacles to mature discipleship, again and again. If something tempts us to spend our money unwisely, or waste our time, or squander our talents and gifts, changes need to be made.

Since we are not perfect, we will always find new obstacles along the way. When we realize we have fallen again, we need to make a change, and empty our spiritual pantries of all those bad cookies. Then we will be on the path again to good stewardship health.

IDEA FOR RESPONSE
Remove 1 thing from your life that hinders you from having a better relationship with Jesus.

TAKE TIME TO REFLECT
What are 3 bad habits I have developed that I need God's help to overcome?

Don't Quit

Then many of his disciples who were listening said, "This saying is hard; who can accept it?" Since Jesus knew that his disciples were murmuring about this, he said to them, "Does this shock you? What if you were to see the Son of Man ascending to where he was before? It is the spirit that gives life, while the flesh is of no avail. The words I have spoken to you are spirit and life. But there are some of you who do not believe." Jesus knew from the beginning the ones who would not believe and the one who would betray him. And he said, "For this reason I have told you that no one can come to me unless it is granted him by my Father." As a result of this, many [of] his disciples returned to their former way of life and no longer accompanied him. Jesus then said to the Twelve, "Do you also want to leave?" Simon Peter answered him, "Master, to whom shall we go? You have the words of eternal life. We have come to believe and are convinced that you are the Holy One of God."

—John 6:60-69

Remember when you joined Weight Watchers way back when? How did that go for you? Remember when you were a student and after the first or second day of that new class you ran to the school office to fill out the slip dropping the class? That was a close one! Then, how about the time you started that Bible study at the parish and after two weeks you disappeared? Who knew there would be actual homework!

If you have never started something and then quit because it was just too difficult or you were scared of what it would ultimately cost, than you are in the minority. I think it is part of the human experience to at some point retreat from that which we find just too much or that which surprised us by the level of difficulty. We were filled with good intentions, but then we decided now was not the time or that we were just incapable of meeting expectations.

Jesus attracted quite a few people in the Gospels. They wanted to be in His presence and follow Him wherever He went. But when He told them what was really entailed in following Him, many "returned to their former way of life." The cost was just too great.

Stewardship calls for us to become mature disciples that respond to Christ's call, regardless of the cost. If we are going to take this commitment seriously, we have to work hard on becoming what we are called to in our baptism. On some days, it might seem easier to drift away or drop out, but this is more important than any class or weight loss program. Those things pass away and we move on, but this journey lasts forever. And better yet, Jesus is willing to tutor us if we let Him.

IDEA FOR RESPONSE
Name 1 thing you really wanted to do but it ended with you giving up. Try again, but this time, allow Jesus into the process by praying frequently.

TAKE TIME TO REFLECT
*What are 3 things in my life I really need
Jesus' help to accomplish?*

Imitating Jesus

So be imitators of God, as beloved children, and live in love, as Christ loved us and handed himself over for us as a sacrificial offering to God for a fragrant aroma.

—Ephesians 5:1-2

Have you ever heard of Wolfgang Beltracchi? For decades he created forgeries of works from the most famous painters in history and he made millions doing it. He was so talented in creating them that many of his creations were hanging, and may even hang to this day, in museums and art galleries around the globe. Experts cannot even tell the difference, and this has led to an inability to verify and then appraise pieces of art all over the world. The risk for the appraiser is too high since they might get it wrong. Beltracchi claims to have made one mistake, using the wrong paint on a painting, which then led to his arrest and conviction. After serving 18 months of a 6-year jail sentence, he continues to create original art and write books in order to help pay for all the lawsuits currently against him.

There is no question about the immorality of lying and cheating in this manner. However, can you even imagine being able to create an imitation of something so close to the original that no one could tell the difference? Someone not familiar with the original could be easily fooled. But to fool so-called experts would be quite amazing.

Saint Paul wrote to the Ephesians and encouraged them to be imitators of Jesus Christ, by living in love and sacrificing their very selves. Can you imagine imitating Jesus so closely that people only see Him when they look at you? The term Christian means to put on Christ. We are to be Jesus Christ to the world, leaving Mass where we have consumed Him in the Eucharist so we can be more like Him. Everyday Stewards are called to give more like Christ, share more like Christ, and love more like Christ. It is no crime to imitate Jesus Christ, but instead, a sin not to try.

IDEA FOR RESPONSE

Go to an art gallery near you and imagine the work and creativity it takes to create some of the pieces that you like.

TAKE TIME TO REFLECT

What are 3 ways in the past week I could have been more Christ-like? What can I do to be more like Christ in those situations in the future?

PUT ON CHRIST

The Risk of Eating Well

So Jesus said to them, "Amen, amen, I say to you, it was not Moses who gave the bread from heaven; my Father gives you the true bread from heaven. For the bread of God is that which comes down from heaven and gives life to the world." So they said to him, "Sir, give us this bread always." Jesus said to them, "I am the bread of life; whoever comes to me will never hunger, and whoever believes in me will never thirst. "

—John 6:32-35

I love watching travel shows hosted by Anthony Bourdain. I can't say I agree with everything in his philosophy of life, but you have to respect someone willing to eat anything, in any part of the world. He demonstrates to his viewers that the world is more interesting and diverse than we allow ourselves to believe. If the Internet makes our world smaller, watching his travels on a television screen makes the world seem big again.

He has a saying that I find very thought provoking: "Good food and good eating are about risk." Giving one's self the chance to discover something new and wonderful sometimes requires us to step outside our comfort zone. We can choose to continue ordering chicken nuggets and mac & cheese just like a child all our lives, or we can risk it and try something from a place outside of our everyday environment.

In the 6th chapter of John's Gospel, Jesus speaks to the crowd about bread that He provides that will take away our hunger for all else in this world. They immediately ask to be given this bread. He responds, "I am the bread of life; whoever comes to me will never hunger, and whoever believes in me will never thirst." What those in the crowd perhaps do not yet understand is that to partake in this bread will entail a great risk! Yes, they will hunger and thirst for nothing else, but they will also enter into a reality filled with trial, temptation, and persecution. They will also be asked to give all they have and live a life totally indebted to Jesus for the sharing of this bread.

But make no mistake, this bread is very good. It is the best, and to partake in the best requires risk. Faithful Christians for two thousand years have proven Anthony Bourdain to be correct.

IDEA FOR RESPONSE

At your next meal, try to be mindful of every bite, noticing taste and texture. Thank God for the experience of eating.

TAKE TIME TO REFLECT

What are 3 things God asks of me that I can find somewhat frightening? How can the Eucharist strengthen me to answer the call?

What Kind of Fool

For Jews demand signs and Greeks look for wisdom, but we proclaim Christ crucified, a stumbling block to Jews and foolishness to Gentiles, but to those who are called, Jews and Greeks alike, Christ the power of God and the wisdom of God. For the foolishness of God is wiser than human wisdom, and the weakness of God is stronger than human strength.

—1 Corinthians 1:22-25

I wonder what some people think of my faith. Actually, most of my friends are people of faith, although not all, and I have worked in the Church all my adult life. My circle seems small against the backdrop of the rest of the world. But, I never shy away from the reality of who I am and I know neighbors and acquaintances know about my faith and how heavily involved I am in it.

I would hope at least for respect. But, they just might think I am certifiably crazy! With the dominance of secularism and the popularity of atheism, I would not be surprised. Spending so much time at parish activities and flying around the country talking about Jesus must seem like a tremendous waste of time.

Paul explains to the Corinthians, "For the foolishness of God is wiser than human wisdom." Everyday stewards are foolish. If you are fortunate enough to have money, possessions, time for endless fun, and marketable talents, to talk about giving that all back to God seems crazy. But our detractors see only with human eyes. When looking through the eyes of faith, we see the greater reality. So Jesus thought He could rebuild the temple in three days? He was insane! You think your daily walk with God will benefit anyone or anything more than running with the worldly pack? You are nuts!

As the world seemingly moves further from God, our foolishness stands out even more. But that is a blessing, because now our foolishness is even more relevant and profound. Just like Jesus in the temple, and Paul preaching of a crucified Christ, our active faith has a huge impact. So let your foolishness stand out. Maybe some out there who want to be fools just need some encouragement and good role models.

IDEA FOR RESPONSE
Dare to be foolish and do something for someone you love that stands out from the norm: create something, sing a song, or buy the person an out of the ordinary gift.

TAKE TIME TO REFLECT

When were 3 times I felt foolish for being a Christian? How did I respond?

We Are Called

After John had been arrested, Jesus came to Galilee proclaiming the gospel of God: "This is the time of fulfillment. The kingdom of God is at hand. Repent, and believe in the gospel." As he passed by the Sea of Galilee, he saw Simon and his brother Andrew casting their nets into the sea; they were fishermen. Jesus said to them, "Come after me, and I will make you fishers of men." Then they abandoned their nets and followed him. He walked along a little farther and saw James, the son of Zebedee, and his brother John. They too were in a boat mending their nets. Then he called them. So they left their father Zebedee in the boat along with the hired men and followed him.

—Mark 1:14-20

I remember when USA Basketball assembled the first "Dream Team" for the 1992 Olympics. Many said it was the greatest sports team ever assembled. In the previous Olympics the US team, made up of college players, only won a bronze medal. There were calls for rules to be amended to allow professional players to play in the games. When the rules were changed, the best NBA players at the time could join the team. They team scored over 100 points in every game and the highest point total allowed by them in a game was 87. The job was to win a gold medal and return the US to world basketball supremacy. They had no problem accomplishing either one.

Usually, if you want to accomplish big goals, you want to assemble the best team possible. However, there are many examples of teams loaded with the best players failing miserably. The most talented or gifted people are not always the right people. Chemistry, attitude, and desire are all components necessary in building a winning team.

We are led to believe that some of those Jesus called to be apostles were not the most talented or smartest people for the job, but they were the right choices. Scripture has these men denying, doubting, and questioning Jesus. But a movement that spread around the world and became the Church was founded on such as these.

God calls each of us to play our part in His plan. We are called from wealth and poverty, from experience and simplicity, and from community and solitude. In Him there is no Greek or Jew, male or female, slave or free. We all are called to be a part and without any one of us, our ability to fulfill that plan is diminished. Call us stewards, disciples, or followers. But whatever name you use, we are all called.

IDEA FOR RESPONSE
Identify 1 aspect of your life, great or small, that needs attention and ask someone you trust in your life to help you.

TAKE TIME TO REFLECT
Who are 3 people in my life that I rely on the most?
What gifts has God given them that I find myself leaning on?

Lessons from Baptizing a Frog

For the love of God is this, that we keep his commandments. And his commandments are not burdensome, for whoever is begotten by God conquers the world. And the victory that conquers the world is our faith. Who [indeed] is the victor over the world but the one who believes that Jesus is the Son of God? This is the one who came through water and blood, Jesus Christ, not by water alone, but by water and blood. The Spirit is the one that testifies, and the Spirit is truth. So there are three that testify, the Spirit, the water, and the blood, and the three are of one accord.

—1 John 5:3-8

I used to lead an RCIA session on baptism where I would bring my Kermit the Frog toy from when I was a child and play baptize it. It was a session I especially made sure I led when we had children preparing for Easter sacraments. You would think Kermit would have become super holy having been baptized so many times, year after year. But, if he had been real, he would not have been any holier due to multiple baptisms then he was after the first baptism. He couldn't be re-baptized. (Not to mention, of course, he is a FROG.)

When Jesus came to John for baptism, he transformed the baptism of repentance that John was practicing into a baptism of redemption. And although we are called to repentance over and over in our life, redemption comes to us only once. We cannot get baptized again in the Jordan or Sea of Galilee because of romantic notions, or come into the Catholic Church by a second baptism so we can start all over. Our baptism, whether we can remember it or not, is a one-time deal. But it is the real deal. Whether you feel it or not, you are sealed for Christ and the stain of original sin has been washed away.

Too many of us take that moment for granted. Yes, you may have been baptized as an infant. But much time has passed since then and you can work to understand the impact that it had on your life. We sometimes look for a good time to begin living a stewardship way of life. However, that time already passed and God has been waiting. We are called to reflect on our baptism and respond to the call it has placed on our lives. We can respond and be disciples, or we can be like Kermit the Frog, always searching for a new start that never comes.

IDEA FOR RESPONSE
Look for your baptismal certificate and place it somewhere of prominence and reflect on what it means to answer your baptismal call.

TAKE TIME TO REFLECT
What are 3 ways I could grow in maturity as a disciple of Jesus Christ?

Recognizing Jesus

So they asked him, "What are you then? Are you Elijah?" And he said, "I am not."
"Are you the Prophet?" He answered, "No." So they said to him, "Who are you,
so we can give an answer to those who sent us? What do you have to say for
yourself?" He said: "I am 'the voice of one crying out in the desert, "Make straight
the way of the Lord,"' as Isaiah the prophet said." Some Pharisees were also sent.
They asked him, "Why then do you baptize if you are not the Messiah or Elijah or
the Prophet?" John answered them, "I baptize with water; but there is one among
you whom you do not recognize, the one who is coming after me, whose sandal
strap I am not worthy to untie."

—John 1:21-27

My wife cannot recognize faces at all. This is true for celebrities as well as acquaintances. It isn't so much that she can't figure out or remember a person's identity, it is that she mistakes people for others all the time. When one of our children or a friend says to my wife, "Oh, look who it is," I have to smile. I don't tease her too much about it, but it is an endless source of amusement for me.

I would guess she might have had a difficult time distinguishing from Elijah, John the Baptist, and Jesus as well, just like those in this reading from the Gospel of John. They asked John the Baptist about who he was on behalf of the Jewish community in Jerusalem. It seemed all very confusing. But John tried to set them straight and explained that he was simply a voice crying out about preparing the way for the Christ. He further explained that the One to come was in their midst, but they did not recognize him.

The Christ in us is sometimes hard to recognize as well. We bear the name Christian, but then by our actions do anything but point towards Jesus Christ. People who do not know Him are left to wonder what all the fuss is about.

It is important to contemplate how well Jesus is reflected in our lives. Are we living like mature disciples and, by our actions, pointing like John the Baptist toward the real Jesus Christ? Do we take the name Christian seriously enough that it changes our lives, so that the One whose name we bear may be seen in us? Recognizing Jesus is not so easy for many, so we really need to help them see clearly. We are called to lead them toward the One whose name we bear.

IDEA FOR RESPONSE
This week go out of your way to assist someone in need, letting the person see Jesus in you.

TAKE TIME TO REFLECT

Who are 3 people that I recognize as "Christ"?
How can I be more like them?

Lost No More

Jesus said to them, "I am the bread of life; whoever comes to me will never hunger, and whoever believes in me will never thirst. But I told you that although you have seen [me], you do not believe. Everything that the Father gives me will come to me, and I will not reject anyone who comes to me, because I came down from heaven not to do my own will but the will of the one who sent me. And this is the will of the one who sent me, that I should not lose anything of what he gave me, but that I should raise it [on] the last day. For this is the will of my Father, that everyone who sees the Son and believes in him may have eternal life, and I shall raise him [on] the last day."

—John 6:35-40

My mother died when I was thirty-one years old. My parents had been married for fifty-five years, and now my father had not only lost his wife, he had lost his identity. He had grown up with three siblings, but they were all deceased. He had been on disability for many years so he had no real job connections left. Yet the biggest part of this identity crisis was he had spent his life as an unbaptized believer.

His brothers and sister had been baptized, but he never knew why he had not. He lived his life feeling like a nobody, which led to drinking and other things lost people do. Whether he never felt good enough or at times didn't care, he never sought out baptism all those years. Maybe he came to Mass with us once at Christmas. But now, he really felt the weight of his years of indecision. He was lost.

Eventually my father moved to be closer to me and began coming to church. After a year or so, he asked me about RCIA. So he began a process in which he probably only understood twenty-five percent of what he heard but he loved one hundred percent of the journey. At the age of seventy-five, Harold Welliver Jr., was baptized and fully initiated into the Catholic Church.

He said this to me, which I will remember and quote forever: "I was someone who didn't belong to anyone or anything, and now I belong." Jesus says in John's Gospel, "And this is the will of the one who sent me, that I should not lose anything of what he gave me, but that I should raise it on the last day." My father passed away three years ago. I miss him every day. He is gone from this world, but he is lost no more.

IDEA FOR RESPONSE
Find your baptismal certificate and place it in a frame. Hang it somewhere in your house where you can regularly see it. It can be for all to see, like in a living room, or only for you, like in a walk-in closet. Let it remind you each time you see it that you belong.

TAKE TIME TO REFLECT

Who are 3 people I know that need to feel a greater sense of belonging? How can I help them, including praying for them?

The Cost of Being a Christian

Three times I begged the Lord about this, that it might leave me, but he said to me, "My grace is sufficient for you, for power is made perfect in weakness." I will rather boast most gladly of my weaknesses, in order that the power of Christ may dwell with me. Therefore, I am content with weaknesses, insults, hardships, persecutions, and constraints, for the sake of Christ; for when I am weak, then I am strong.

—2 Corinthians 12:8-10

There was an article in an October 2013 article in the UK magazine, *The Spectator*, entitled, "The War on Christians." The article was a reflection on the fact that the growing global persecution of Christians is either unreported or under-reported by most media outlets. This was written in 2013, even before ISIS and much of the systematic execution of Christians in Syria and Iraq. John L. Allen Jr. reported in the article that a study found that in the decade before 2013, at least 100,000 Christians had been killed because of their faith. He wrote, "That works out to 11 Christians killed somewhere in the world every hour, seven days a week and 365 days a year."

In Paul's Second Letter to the Corinthians, he wrote about his weaknesses and his persecutions and insults. He witnessed to the fact that through his suffering of these things for the sake of Christ, his weakness became strength. It is so hard to hear Paul's words while reading a report of mass killings or seeing a video of someone approaching martyrdom, especially if the mainstream media sees it as just another news story.

But in the 21st century, Christians are under attack in a big way. In stewardship spirituality we talk about a mature discipleship where we respond to Christ's call, no matter the cost. Well, in today's world the cost is getting greater and greater. But our strength is in Jesus and the Body of Christ. All our trials and persecutions are connected, whether big or small. Solidarity helped bring down Communism in much of the world and, today, together we can stand with all our Christian brothers and sisters in the face of new evils. It is very hard, of course, but in this battle the victory is already won.

http://www.spectator.co.uk/features/9041841/the-war-on-christians/

IDEA FOR RESPONSE
Spend 1 hour this week becoming familiar with the various ways Christians are being persecuted throughout the world. Search out stories in secular media and Christian media, such as Catholic News Service.

TAKE TIME TO REFLECT
In what way have I ever felt persecuted by others because of my Catholic faith?

PERSECUTION

Be Accountable

The 6th Characteristic
of an Everyday Steward

Resembling Jesus

See what love the Father has bestowed on us that we may be called the children of God. Yet so we are. The reason the world does not know us is that it did not know him. Beloved, we are God's children now; what we shall be has not yet been revealed. We do know that when it is revealed we shall be like him, for we shall see him as he is.

—1 John 3:1-2

I was putting together one of those online holiday video greetings, the ones where you place photos of people's faces onto animated bodies. The video featured five characters, perfect for our family of two parents and three children. After importing the faces and finalizing the video, I hit play and sat back to watch it. After watching about 25% of the video clip, I wondered why my oldest son was not appearing on the screen. Then I realized in amazement, I didn't recognize him because I had mistaken his face for mine! Without bodies, our faces looked so alike and I couldn't tell the difference at first.

The First Letter of John tells us that the world does not yet see us for who we are because it does not recognize Jesus. When the world finally recognizes Jesus, all will see us for who we are because we will look like Him. So for now, do not assume people will look at you and say, "What a great steward and disciple! You are just like Jesus!" Some will see your way of life and understand. They will be inspired to be like Jesus as well. But many will look at you and listen to what you have to say and actually wonder why you don't wake up and conform to the world. It is not easy when you find yourself in the situation that you are the only intentional disciple in your neighborhood, at work, or even in your family. This is especially difficult when you are young and in school environments when God is a subject and not a reality.

But fear not! You are not alone! And when the time comes to pass when all creation sees Him for whom He really is, they will find it hard to tell Him and His children apart. In fact, I wouldn't want to resemble anybody else.

IDEA FOR RESPONSE

Ask someone close to you if he or she has ever seen Christ through you and have the person elaborate.

TAKE TIME TO REFLECT

When was the last time I saw the face of Christ in someone else?

Stepping Up to the Plate

What good is it, my brothers, if someone says he has faith but does not have works? Can that faith save him? If a brother or sister has nothing to wear and has no food for the day and one of you says to them, "Go in peace, keep warm, and eat well," but you do not give them the necessities of the body, what good is it? So also faith of itself, if it does not have works, is dead. Indeed someone might say, "You have faith and I have works." Demonstrate your faith to me without works, and I will demonstrate my faith to you from my works.

—James 2:14-18

I am sure I drive my kids crazy! When they fail to do, over and over again, that which I have asked them to do, they continue to say, "I'm sorry," to which I say, "No, you're not!" They look at me with that look that says, "How can you not accept my apology? Who doesn't accept 'I'm sorry?'" Then I say to them, "If you were truly sorry you would change and do what I asked you to do!" Of course, their response almost always is, "I forgot!" Forgot? How does someone forget something that has been asked of him or her several times in the course of day? Well, if I drive them crazy, I am sure it is because they drove me crazy first!

Saint James would probably be on my side, or at least I want to believe he would. He asked the question, "What good is it if someone says he has faith but does not have works?" He goes on to speak about those who would wish another well, only to do nothing to help the other to be well. Unfortunately, all of us sometimes fall into the trap of talking a good game but not really stepping up to the plate to do something. We say all the right things, but then do much less than what is required, or even nothing at all.

It isn't easy being a good steward, daily answering the call to share more, give more, and love more. Even when I write these reflections, I am struck by my own shortcomings and failings. I don't want to just write something and not internalize it to the point where I must act. As an Everyday Steward, I strive to at least be a better disciple this day than I was the last, and pray to be better tomorrow than I am today. I guess if I can just ask that of my kids as well, they might not see me as so crazy after all.

IDEA FOR RESPONSE
Think of something that you failed to follow through on and do what it takes to complete the task.

TAKE TIME TO REFLECT
What are 3 things that cause me to procrastinate in everyday life? How can God help me overcome these things?

DO SOMETHING

This Little Light of Mine

And this is the verdict, that the light came into the world, but people preferred darkness to light, because their works were evil. For everyone who does wicked things hates the light and does not come toward the light, so that his works might not be exposed. But whoever lives the truth comes to the light, so that his works may be clearly seen as done in God.

—John 3:19-21

My pastor collects old paschal candles. They never stand as profoundly as they did when first brought out at Easter. However, the burnt wicks and melted wax represent the many lives made new in baptism, the faithful who have passed into the next life, and the glory and grandeur of another Easter Vigil and Easter season.

When entering a room with much history, we often reflect, "If only these walls could talk." What if a paschal candle could speak? It would tell us of each life that was filled with darkness until the light of Christ entered into them. It would tell us of infants who received the promise of eternal life through their parents' faith and testimony. We would hear of adults who once were lost and wandering and how now they were found. It would share with us the stories of pain and suffering that ended in the loving arms of Jesus Christ at death. It would tell us all of these things, and would also remind us that it existed to attest to the truth of the Light, that through that Light all things might be seen more clearly.

Do you have your baptismal candle close by? It has shared a flame with one of these paschal candles. It attests to the truth that the Light still resides in you. Bring it out and light it once more. Use it to pray and reflect on your life. Ask the Lord to grow that Light inside you, that all around you may see it. By this Light you have been able to see more clearly. By the Light shining more brightly in you, others might be able to see more clearly as well.

IDEA FOR RESPONSE

Find your baptismal candle and light it for 5 minutes of prayer.

TAKE TIME TO REFLECT

What are 3 obstacles in my life that prevent my light from shining more brightly?

SHINE BRIGHT

All Families Are Holy

A father's glory is glory also for oneself; they multiply sin who demean their mother. My son, be steadfast in honoring your father; do not grieve him as long as he lives. Even if his mind fails, be considerate of him; do not revile him because you are in your prime. Kindness to a father will not be forgotten; it will serve as a sin offering—it will take lasting root. In time of trouble it will be recalled to your advantage, like warmth upon frost it will melt away your sins.

—Sirach 3:11-15

I need to read to my children the passage from Sirach that talks about children and their responsibilities toward their parents. It talks about obedience, consideration, and kindness. But I particularly want them to hear the verse translated in the Revised Lectionary, "take care of your father when he is old." I am hoping for a little bungalow by the ocean with a fully stocked pantry, fridge, and bar.

But seriously, scripture points out to us that those in a family have responsibilities for each other. Most of us don't choose our family. However, we do choose whether or not to fulfill those responsibilities.

When I began really getting into stewardship spirituality, my entire view of my children changed. No longer did I just love them because they happened to be born to my wife and me. They were true gifts, entrusted to us by God. The crux of the change came when I realized I would be accountable for how I received these gifts and helped mold them into something more. I no longer saw them as mine, but His.

My eyes tear up almost every time I really reflect on this reality. Amazingly, I love them more now after realizing they aren't really mine. I think it is because I see in them now more than ever God's own likeness. Also, I feel most humbled that God should see fit to entrust these three amazing creations of His to little ol' me.

Now, more than ever, we need to pray for families in our world. The family is under attack from every side, and every force great and small. If we can begin to see the true gifts we are to one another, than our actions will speak that truth. If we can see the responsibility we have for each other, then we can show the world the true meaning of love.

IDEA FOR RESPONSE
Pick up the phone today and call someone in your family you do not see everyday and tell the person how much you love him or her.

TAKE TIME TO REFLECT
Who are 3 members of my family or 3 close friends that God has used in my life to bring me closer to Him?

Knowing Your Gifts

"It will be as when a man who was going on a journey called in his servants and entrusted his possessions to them. To one he gave five talents; to another, two; to a third, one—to each according to his ability. Then he went away. Immediately the one who received five talents went and traded with them, and made another five. Likewise, the one who received two made another two. But the man who received one went off and dug a hole in the ground and buried his master's money."

—Matthew 25:14-18

The quintessential stewardship parable that Jesus told is the parable of the talents. We can take for granted the reality that we should use that which God has given us and grow it more abundantly to offer it back to God. But I feel for the fearful servant who was too afraid to do much with the one talent he was given. I think he was afraid, not just because of the demands of the master, but because he had no real idea how to grow one talent into anything. He was really unaware of what he had been given.

One day I was teaching a class on giftedness and strengths. I said that we know when we are using the gifts God gave us because we are happiest at those times. A woman immediately shared with the group she was giving up reading at Mass. I asked why, because I thought she was good at it. She said every time she has to read she leaves the house with knots in her stomach. She felt that even though she had found a way to compensate, this was not God's gift to her. Weeks later she found me at Mass and grabbed my arm, saying, "Today is my first day as an Extraordinary Minister of Holy Communion and I left the house happy as can be! Thank you!"

How can you be a good steward when you don't know what God has given you? Many are in that situation. I truly believe that we are created so uniquely that we may have that one talent that no one else has been given. The other servants in the story made more from what they had been given. But the fearful servant may have been given the one talent that he could have grown into a fortune.

IDEA FOR RESPONSE
If you have never taken it before, take the Clifton StrengthsFinder assessment online. Codes can be purchased online or can be found in several books from Gallup.

TAKE TIME TO REFLECT

What are 3 characteristics that make me special?
What do I regularly do to grow those into real strengths to use for God's glory?

At the End of the Day, Whom Do You Serve?

For the sake of Jacob, my servant, of Israel my chosen one,
I have called you by name, giving you a title, though you do not know me.
I am the LORD, there is no other, there is no God besides me.
It is I who arm you, though you do not know me,
so that all may know, from the rising of the sun
to its setting, that there is none besides me.
I am the LORD, there is no other.

—Isaiah 45:4-6

Years ago Bob Dylan wrote, "You're gonna have to serve somebody." The fact that you and I are Americans (most of us anyway), work jobs to provide for ourselves and our families, maybe belong to civic organizations, have membership in a parish, and ultimately identify ourselves as Christian means we have many things that vie for our time, talent, and treasure. But Mr. Dylan points out that regardless of all the labels we wear in this earthly life, those labels do not determine whom we ultimately serve.

I have worked for the Catholic Church for over twenty years. I have worked for multiple pastors. I also have been privileged enough to travel to many places to teach and give presentations on faith, stewardship, and engagement at the request of more pastors and bishops. I have always tried to do my very best for those who seek to employ me, not just because they are paying good money, but because they represent Jesus Christ's church. But every day, no matter where I may be, the sun sets and eventually my day ends, and I am aware that it is just me and Jesus. And the question I try to ask myself each day, unless I am so tired I have already fallen asleep before my head hits the pillow, is: "Have I pleased you today, Lord?"

So, yes, pay to Caesar what Caesar says is his. Participate in all those things that God provides on earth to give order in our lives. Work your job to the best of your ability and let that work glorify him. Fully participate in your parish, realizing that through that entity you have access to the real living God in the sacraments. But never lose sight of the words of God in Isaiah, "I am the LORD, there is no other."

IDEA FOR RESPONSE
When you go to bed tonight, ask God the question, "Have I pleased you today, Lord?" Then spend 5–10 minutes examining the events of the day.

TAKE TIME TO REFLECT
What are 3 obstacles present in my life preventing me from serving God alone?

New Creation Versus Human Nature

For the love of Christ impels us, once we have come to the conviction that one died for all; therefore, all have died. He indeed died for all, so that those who live might no longer live for themselves but for him who for their sake died and was raised.

Consequently, from now on we regard no one according to the flesh; even if we once knew Christ according to the flesh, yet now we know him so no longer. So whoever is in Christ is a new creation: the old things have passed away; behold, new things have come.

— 2 Corinthians 5:14-17

It would appear that many in the modern world think very little of human nature. If we are to believe print, television, and online media, apparently we are unable to control our lust for people, power, and money and, if given a choice, we will choose incorrectly most of the time. Worse than that assessment, because this is seen as truth, those choices actually are no longer that bad. How can something be bad if everyone is doing it? Come to think of it, this argument is not just from the media world; I hear it from my own children from time to time. Honestly, as my children get older and their arguments wiser, I find myself wondering if certain things really are not as I once saw them.

But then I remember who I am as a baptized person: a new creation in Jesus Christ. The reality is the world is right: I can't control my lust for things and, yes, many times if given the chance I will choose incorrectly. But this is without Jesus. With Jesus, I have been transformed and given the power to resist temptation and follow a narrow, but better, way. To be a good steward, a mature disciple, and relevant Christian, we must have Jesus. My children and I sometimes fail to see that those who seek to reduce human actions to simple animalistic responses to a stimulus also reduce the dignity of the human person. We are so much more than that. Through His cross and resurrection, Jesus redeemed all of creation. And for those who seek to join His body here on earth, these words of Paul are for us: "So whoever is in Christ is a new creation: the old things have passed away; behold, new things have come."

IDEA FOR RESPONSE

Either memorize or write down on a small card the words of Paul at the end of this entry. When you find yourself in moments of lust for money, possessions, or a person, say these words quietly to yourself.

TAKE TIME TO REFLECT

What are 3 aspects of my life where I have not allowed the power of my baptism to enter? What steps can I take to change this reality?

Liturgical Year

Your Seasonal Journey

Advent I – Your Last Advent on Earth

"Be watchful! Be alert! You do not know when the time will come. It is like a man traveling abroad. He leaves home and places his servants in charge, each with his work, and orders the gatekeeper to be on the watch. Watch, therefore; you do not know when the lord of the house is coming, whether in the evening, or at midnight, or at cockcrow, or in the morning. May he not come suddenly and find you sleeping. What I say to you, I say to all: 'Watch!'"

—Mark 13:33-37

Waiting is not always so easy. If you lack patience, like me, you probably want whatever is going to happen to just happen already. I remember waiting on the births of my children. There was the time I sat with my dying father in the hospital. Last year we waited to see if our oldest child got into the college of his choice, or any college at all, which seemed quite nerve-wracking.

So, to make the time pass more easily, and because it is prudent and wise, we make preparations. We put together nurseries, go over last will and testaments, and look through endless college mailings. Then, when the event finally happens or our fate is unveiled, the preparation ends. Either you have prepared well for that moment, or you realize your actions didn't prepare you at all.

Advent comes every year. So, unlike events in our lives that only happen once, we have been through Advent many times before. Even though this is the case, when Christmas arrives many of us will think we missed it again and next year will be the year we really get into Advent. Of course, not to sound morbid, but there is no promise of next year. What if you knew this was your last Advent ever?

I read a book some years ago about how to live your life as if you only had one year to live. The author said that doing this provides incentive for a real commitment to living life to its fullest. You notice things for the first time. You make those plans that you always put off. You tell people what you always wanted to say.

I hope all who read this have many wonderful years ahead of them. However, let's approach this Advent like it is our last. I bet Christmas will seem that much sweeter. And who knows, we may find a new and improved way to live all year long.

IDEA FOR RESPONSE
Buy two Advent wreaths. If you do not have one, place one on your table and use it. Give the second one away to a friend. If you already have one, give them both away.

TAKE TIME TO REFLECT
If I only had 1 year to live, what would be the top 3 changes in my life to make?

Advent II – Preparing by Doing Nothing

But do not ignore this one fact, beloved, that with the Lord one day is like a thousand years and a thousand years like one day. The Lord does not delay his promise, as some regard "delay," but he is patient with you, not wishing that any should perish but that all should come to repentance.

—2 Peter 3:8-9

I like sleeping on a long trip when somebody else is driving. You fall asleep at one point on the trip and wake up maybe 90 minutes later and—surprise—90 minutes gone in what seems like 1 is awesome!

Time never changes for us, but how we perceive its passing does. Children are easily bored after just a few minutes of waiting for something. Sometimes, things seem to happen too quickly, leaving us feeling unprepared.

Yes, I believe that God gives meaning to our life. But I also think the singer and songwriter James Taylor had it right when he wrote the lyric, "The secret of life is enjoying the passage of time." When we are busy with work, family, church, or the normal events of daily life we can easily feel purpose in our lives. It is when nothing is happening we sometimes wonder if the world is passing us by.

Good stewards are called to give all time back to God. It is easy to see why we would give Him the good times and, of course, call on Him in the bad times. But we need to give Him the ordinary quiet times as well. We need to revel in the gift of just passing some time sitting on a porch, or waiting for a phone call, or reflecting on the day before heading to bed. I will admit I am sometimes at my best when I am doing nothing. Sounds strange, I know. But I am more keenly aware at those times that Jesus is close to me. I am always better when I am by God's side.

So, this Advent, watch and wait. He is coming soon. The secret is enjoying the wait.

IDEA FOR RESPONSE
Take 20 minutes and sit on your front porch or in a park and just observe all of God's creation around you.

TAKE TIME TO REFLECT

What are 3 things I am waiting for that really test my patience? How can this Scripture reading and reflection help me?

PATIENCE

Christmas – The Disruption of the Incarnation

For it says in scripture: "Behold, I am laying a stone in Zion, a cornerstone, chosen and precious, and whoever believes in it shall not be put to shame." Therefore, its value is for you who have faith, but for those without faith: "The stone which the builders rejected has become the cornerstone," and "A stone that will make people stumble, and a rock that will make them fall." They stumble by disobeying the word, as is their destiny. But you are "a chosen race, a royal priesthood, a holy nation, a people of his own, so that you may announce the praises" of him who called you out of darkness into his wonderful light.

—1 Peter 2:6-9

One December my oldest son informed us a he would be getting up early on Christmas morning to serve breakfast to homeless people at the nearby shelter. We are a good Christian family but we never before had that tradition. Christmas had been always the same: go to Mass on Christmas Eve, get up early, open presents, reflect briefly on the fact the day was a birthday celebration for Jesus, and then I would run off to my job, back at the Church. My family always went on Christmas Eve so I was a lone ranger on Christmas Day. But this year, my son threw a wrench into the plan.

I can't say his siblings were too happy at first. When they woke up, he would be gone. If that were not bad enough, that our family wasn't together at the crack of dawn on Christmas morning, they would have to wait to open presents until his return. It seemed that this wasn't about serving the poor at all! It seemed to them it was my son making Christmas morning all about him!

I couldn't be mad at my other children for feeling the way they did. It was a natural human response. When our routine is disrupted, we feel uneasy. When our expectations are not met, we feel a little cheated. When others stand in our way of happiness, even if they just delay it for a bit, we feel impatient. Of course, he went to the soup kitchen, and when he returned everything unfolded as it usually does. And we were all proud of him.

The call of Jesus Christ often disrupts our routines, changes our expectations, and pulls us out of our comfort zone. The story of Christmas is anything but a story of ordinary happenings. May we continue to allow the God who knelt down to earth in a lowly stable to disrupt our lives for the Kingdom of God.

IDEA FOR RESPONSE

This Christmas, decide to spend at least an hour or two helping feed the homeless, imprisoned, elderly, or lonely.

TAKE TIME TO REFLECT

What 3 things can I add to my Christmas season routine that would help me become a better Everyday Steward?

DISRUPTION

Ash Wednesday – Bearing the Mark of Jesus

So we are ambassadors for Christ, as if God were appealing through us. We implore you on behalf of Christ, be reconciled to God. For our sake he made him to be sin who did not know sin, so that we might become the righteousness of God in him.

—2 Corinthians 5:20-21

I remember one year when Ash Wednesday and a presidential debate fell on the same day. Knowing there were a few Catholics involved, I waited to see if any would appear with ashes on their forehead on national television. Alas, none of them did. And of course, there was no mention of it being Ash Wednesday.

It is not a holy day of obligation so maybe no one went to Mass that day. Or maybe they did and after reading Jesus' admonishment of the hypocrites showing off their fasting, prayers, and almsgiving they decided to wash their foreheads. I certainly would never question people's faith by whether or not they still had ashes on their head.

However, we do allow the words of Jesus to serve as an excuse to play down our faith. I don't think that ever was His intention. Bearing witness and showing off are two different things. I personally love to see all the area high school kids at Mass on Ash Wednesday before school. And I know firsthand that most of them wear those ashes all day long and are asked several times what that smudge on their head is all about. Believe me, when you are 16 years old that is not showing off. That's courage.

Ash Wednesday is a perfect day to bring God into the everyday places and moments of life. Whether you happen to be on television or in a grocery store, those ashes say more than any amount of words. If you can get to Mass early, they will be there all day. So, you say evangelization is difficult and not for you? On Ash Wednesday the Church makes it easy for you.

IDEA FOR RESPONSE

Find 1 additional way you can bear witness to the role Jesus Christ plays in your life: a cross, a piece of art, a bumper sticker, a t-shirt, etc.

TAKE TIME TO REFLECT

When were 3 times I was apprehensive or uncomfortable to share my faith?

EVANGELIZE

Lent I - Dying to Ourselves

Amen, amen, I say to you, unless a grain of wheat falls to the ground and dies, it remains just a grain of wheat; but if it dies, it produces much fruit. Whoever loves his life loses it, and whoever hates his life in this world will preserve it for eternal life. Whoever serves me must follow me, and where I am, there also will my servant be. The Father will honor whoever serves me.

—John 12:24-26

Every Lent, a reflection on the power of the cross can bring a person to tears. To endure such pain and anguish in order to bring new life to a fallen world is an unfathomable event in salvation history. With blood and tears filling His eyes, Jesus cries out, "Why have you forsaken me?" Make no mistake; the Incarnation rests broken on an executioner's wooden device of torture made from hate and ridicule. Yet out of this experience, all things are made new.

Jesus was that grain of wheat that fell to the ground and died, but an endless supply of fruit has been produced. When Jesus spoke about the time when He would be glorified, He tried to explain how this process of new life works. An old life must end for a new one to begin. His dying and rising took place exactly for the purpose of providing us a way of dying and rising in Him.

Stewardship calls for us to die to ourselves and live new lives in Jesus Christ. Like grains of wheat that fall to the ground, we can now produce much fruit. If we do not die to ourselves, we remain unchanged and unable to share in His abundance of grace.

With Lent drawing to a close, there is still time to make sure the old self is gone. Find time to go to the sacrament of penance. Take part in the extra devotions in your parish, such as Stations of the Cross or Eucharistic adoration. Spend more personal time in prayer. Then, when Easter comes, the fruit that has been and will be produced can be offered to God. Your gifts will be received with great joy and they will be multiplied.

For we have died and risen with Jesus Christ, so that we shall not die again.

IDEA FOR RESPONSE
Find time to receive the sacrament of penance in the coming weeks.

TAKE TIME TO REFLECT

What is 1 Catholic devotion that I could learn more about and possibly add to my prayer life?

LIFE IN CHRIST

Lent II – Carrying the Cross

At noon darkness came over the whole land until three in the afternoon. And at three o'clock Jesus cried out in a loud voice, "Eloi, Eloi, lema sabachthani?" which is translated, "My God, my God, why have you forsaken me?" Some of the bystanders who heard it said, "Look, he is calling Elijah." One of them ran, soaked a sponge with wine, put it on a reed, and gave it to him to drink, saying, "Wait, let us see if Elijah comes to take him down." Jesus gave a loud cry and breathed his last.

—Mark 15:33-37

In trying to understand the true power of stewardship, we need not look any further than the cross. It serves as a tremendous example of giving everything away freely for God and the people of God. Jesus answered the call, regardless of the cost, and the cost was life itself.

Most of us will never have to sacrifice our lives in response to God's call. But there are Christians all across the globe that do every day. Missionaries have died due to violence or disease. Activists stood up for the basic rights of others and have lost their own right to live. Men and women who swore to keep the peace or rescue others from disaster have traded a lifetime with family and friends for the sake of the vulnerable. These people answered that call and responded with courage and commitment.

But even though our sacrifice might not be as great, it does not diminish the power in the response. Perhaps through our small everyday actions, someone will be touched by God and then transformed. It is not the size of the sacrifice that counts, but the complete willingness to give that sacrifice. Jesus' sacrifice is sufficient for the salvation of all humanity. Now, we are called to translate that reality into our own somewhat simple lives.

On those days when being a good steward seems too difficult, look to the cross and find strength in a God who knows how hard this earthly life can be at times. Look to fellow stewards who are carrying their crosses and find empathy and companionship. Reflect on the lives of saints and those who gave their lives because of their love of God. Then go forth into a world that so badly needs Jesus and give thanks for knowing how hard the day otherwise would be without Him.

IDEA FOR RESPONSE
Find a copy of *The Passion* or *Jesus of Nazareth* and watch again the scenes of Jesus' passion and death.

TAKE TIME TO REFLECT
What do I have in time, talent, or treasure that I have yet to freely give back to God?

THE CROSS

Holy Thursday – Washing Each Other's Feet

He took a towel and tied it around his waist. Then he poured water into a basin and began to wash the disciples' feet and dry them with the towel around his waist. He came to Simon Peter, who said to him, "Master, are you going to wash my feet?" Jesus answered and said to him, "What I am doing, you do not understand now, but you will understand later." Peter said to him, "You will never wash my feet." Jesus answered him, "Unless I wash you, you will have no inheritance with me." Simon Peter said to him, "Master, then not only my feet, but my hands and head as well."

So when he had washed their feet [and] put his garments back on and reclined at table again, he said to them, "Do you realize what I have done for you? You call me 'teacher' and 'master,' and rightly so, for indeed I am. If I, therefore, the master and teacher, have washed your feet, you ought to wash one another's feet. I have given you a model to follow, so that as I have done for you, you should also do.

—John 13:4b-9,12-15

Christian stewardship began this night in the upper room. Ordinary humans witnessed the Son of God humble himself to a point they could not have imagined, all with the purpose of serving them. That night the ordinary became extraordinary. Jesus demonstrated for them true love and how to share that love with those outside that room. But how could they win hearts for Jesus when they saw themselves as so much less than their teacher? The answer was He would then feed them with His very self. They would not see Him much longer, for the events that began with that evening would lead to His torture, death, resurrection, and then ascension to the Father. But in His Body & Blood they would be nourished for the task at hand: to witness to the whole world the Good News of Jesus Christ.

In one night, Jesus gave us a true example of stewardship and the path to follow. By His example He showed us how to empty ourselves to the point of becoming the servant of all. The path is the Holy Eucharist, through which all is possible. When we partake in his banquet, we become Christ to a world in need of Christ. It would be a truly daunting task if He hadn't shown us how *to be Christ*. But a simple act of washing feet taught us more than any sermon or sacred writing.

As good stewards we believe all we have is a gift from God. That night, before the institution of the Eucharist, Jesus commanded us to wash each other's feet. In essence, He gave us to one another. If we claim to belong to Him, then we by definition belong to each other. May the Christ in each of us propel us to our knees so that we may never stop washing each other's feet.

IDEA FOR RESPONSE
Find a time and place in the coming week for at least 10 minutes of Eucharistic Adoration.

TAKE TIME TO REFLECT

*What are 3 ways I **am Christ** to people on a regular basis?*

The Passion – Take Up Your Cross & Follow Me

Then Jesus said to his disciples, "Whoever wishes to come after me must deny himself, take up his cross, and follow me. For whoever wishes to save his life will lose it, but whoever loses his life for my sake will find it. What profit would there be for one to gain the whole world and forfeit his life? Or what can one give in exchange for his life?

—Matthew 24-26

Jesus warns us in the Gospel of Matthew, "If anyone wishes to come after me, he must deny himself, take up his cross, and follow me." It is an invitation to a way of life, and a plan that leads to holiness, but make no mistake, it is a warning as well. The cross is a sign of victory, but only in light of the Resurrection. Alone, it is a symbol of ultimate sacrifice: the sacrifice of Jesus Christ for a fallen world, and the sacrifice we are called to make to truly follow Him.

The power of this symbol has been diminished in popular culture. It is often used in fashion, simple wall art, and on bumper stickers and t-shirts, sometimes with Christian clichés, and sometimes not. But the cross is something so much more. It is a reminder of the pain, suffering, and death of One who loved us so much, He would give His very life for us. It is our God on that cross. It is God who cries out in despair, feeling the ultimate depth of human emotion. And there lies the key for us in trying to live this life of carrying our crosses.

For those who suffer the death of a loved one, the Father lost his Son. For those who suffer the ravages of disease, His body was broken, beaten, and pierced. For those who feel they have no way out, whether due to prisons that are physical or prisons that are of the mind, He hung on a cross and cried out, "Why?" For those who feel alone and abandoned, He hung on a tree where no one could comfort Him, not even His own mother. He has walked in all our shoes, and now we are called to walk in His. In the cross, we find solidarity with the human condition. In an empty tomb, we find our hope.

IDEA FOR RESPONSE

Find a cross or crucifix in your home, look at it, and reflect on what it is saying to you.

TAKE TIME TO REFLECT

When was a recent time when God asked me to sacrifice and I was less than willing?

SOLIDARITY

Easter Vigil – Illuminating Our Darkness

In the beginning, when God created the heavens and the earth — and the earth was without form or shape, with darkness over the abyss and a mighty wind sweeping over the waters — Then God said: Let there be light, and there was light. God saw that the light was good. God then separated the light from the darkness.

—Genesis 1:1-4

The light of a single candle can illuminate an entire room. The strike of a match suddenly chases away the darkness, allowing you to see all around. However, if you move about too quickly while carrying the candle, the flame may go out. You can bend your hand around the flame to protect it from the seemingly innocent breeze as you walk, but it will still dance about as if it is warning you it is about to expire.

So you light another candle. One you will carry and the other you set on the table. There is now even more light, but more importantly, you are assured if the flame you carry dies out, the candle on the table will remain lit. However, a candle does not last forever. The wax will melt away, little by little, making you wonder if darkness will engulf you before the sun rises again. So you rely on new candles throughout the night. One candle breaks through the darkness, but multiple candles ensure that the light brought about by the first one will not disappear.

At Easter Vigil liturgies around the globe, new paschal and processional candles will illuminate the night as new stewards are baptized and current stewards renew promises made years ago. The sun will rise on Easter Sunday morning and the need for candle flames will be no more. May the Light of Christ that burns in each of us combine to brighten the entire world so that all may see, until the Son appears once again, just like on that first Easter Morning.

IDEA FOR RESPONSE
Spend 10 minutes in a completely darkened room and imagine a world without light.

TAKE TIME TO REFLECT
Who are 3 people that need the Light of Christ in their lives and how can I help bring that to them?

Easter Sunday – The Necessity of an Empty Tomb

When they looked up, they saw that the stone had been rolled back; it was very large. On entering the tomb they saw a young man sitting on the right side, clothed in a white robe, and they were utterly amazed. He said to them, "Do not be amazed! You seek Jesus of Nazareth, the crucified. He has been raised; he is not here. Behold the place where they laid him. But go and tell his disciples and Peter, 'He is going before you to Galilee; there you will see him, as he told you.'"

—Mark 16:4-7

When I married my wife, I also inherited her family tradition of having pennies lead the way to each child's basket on Easter Sunday morning. I had never encountered such a thing. When I was a child, the basket was just there. There was no journey, no path, and no pennies. Today, even with children older and more mature, at least in their minds, the pennies are still there. The destination is great, but the journey makes it that much better.

Lent is now over. The journey was long and at times, not easy. However, Easter does not exist without Good Friday. The Resurrection does not have the same impact without the Passion. To get anywhere of value and importance, there is always a journey to get there.

But now, the real journey begins. We are an Easter people and now we are called to live out our baptismal call. In baptism, we died and rose with Christ. The story of Lent is our story, and the incredible plot twist of Easter belongs to our story as well.

If Jesus did not rise from the dead, there is no need for stewardship. Without a crucified and risen Lord, we still need to help one another, show kindness, and be people of virtue. These actions help to make a civilized society work. But with an empty tomb, we do these basic actions, and so much more, because now we have a hope in something beyond our earthly lives, something that eternally lasts. We are an Easter people!

A new meaning has been given to our very existence because of this Good News.

So with Easter, the journey has only begun. There aren't pennies to guide the way, but a risen Savior that now walks with us, from this world into the next. Alleluia! Alleluia!

IDEA FOR RESPONSE
Take the time to reread the Gospel accounts of the Resurrection, this time being more mindful of the reality of the event.

TAKE TIME TO REFLECT

What difference does it make in my life that Jesus is really alive?

ALLELUIA!

Mary

Your Companion
for the Journey

Bearing God to the World

During those days Mary set out and traveled to the hill country in haste to a town of Judah, where she entered the house of Zechariah and greeted Elizabeth. When Elizabeth heard Mary's greeting, the infant leaped in her womb, and Elizabeth, filled with the holy Spirit, cried out in a loud voice and said, "Most blessed are you among women, and blessed is the fruit of your womb. And how does this happen to me, that the mother of my Lord should come to me? For at the moment the sound of your greeting reached my ears, the infant in my womb leaped for joy. Blessed are you who believed that what was spoken to you by the Lord would be fulfilled."

—Luke 1:39-45

T*heotokos* is a term used primarily in the East for Our Lady, literally meaning "God-bearer." The theological reality implied in the name is that Mary truly carried in her womb, and then gave birth to, the Incarnation, God in human form. So, we in the West usually translate the word into "Mother of God."

However, let's look at the word for it's more literal meaning. Mary bore Jesus, that is carried Him inside herself, until she gave birth to Him in a manger. The emphasis is not only on the birth, but also the actual time of pregnancy. For 9 months, all who came into contact with her were in the real presence of the Divine. Recall her visit to see her cousin, Elizabeth. The child in Elizabeth's womb, John the Baptist, started leaping with joy to be in the presence of God in Mary's womb.

Mary serves as an example to us on how to live holy lives. But, we are also called to be "God-bearers." Because of her *fiat*, her saying yes to God's plan of salvation, Jesus Christ entered the world. He remains with us, most notably in the sacrament of Eucharist. When we go forth from Mass, we bear God within us, taking Him into the world. All that come into contact with us are in the real presence of the Divine.

All this is possible because Mary totally gave herself over to God. As good stewards, we are called to do the same. When we say yes, we then receive Jesus in the sacraments. We then carry Him into a world that needs the presence of the Divine more than ever. Our calendar year begins with a reminder of this reality, the Solemnity of Mary, the Holy Mother of God. A good resolution for this New Year is to try hard to bring God to others, just as Mary did for us. May our devotion to her, as Theotokos, be our constant reminder to be *theotokos* to others.

IDEA FOR RESPONSE
Say a rosary for the intention of those you know who need to feel the presence of God in their life the most.

TAKE TIME TO REFLECT
Who are 3 people who have brought the love of Jesus Christ to me?

Our Human Destiny

In him we were also chosen, destined in accord with the purpose of the One who accomplishes all things according to the intention of his will, so that we might exist for the praise of his glory, we who first hoped in Christ. In him you also, who have heard the word of truth, the gospel of your salvation, and have believed in him, were sealed with the promised holy Spirit, which is the first installment of our inheritance toward redemption as God's possession, to the praise of his glory.

—Ephesians 1:11-14

Saint John Paul II, on the feast of the Immaculate Conception, wrote in his homily, "sanctifying grace is, in fact, the divine life as grafted into the human soul." We begin life without this grace due to original sin, but Mary was conceived without original sin, and therefore, had this grace at her conception. Saint John Paul II points out that Mary then was able to concern herself with our redemption and say yes to being the Mother of God in a "perfect and universal manner," since she did not need to focus that energy on herself. We are then to follow her example and use the gift of grace that we receive through the sacraments and Jesus' redemptive action of His passion to bring about the Kingdom of God.

For Everyday Stewards, this is pretty heady stuff, but also very important. The modern canonized saint uses this theology to impress upon us the importance of not becoming cultural Catholics, but committed disciples instead. He wrote the quoted homily in 1959, and that warning against the *relegation of faith* sounds even more urgent today. Mary's existence was key to God's plan of redemption. It was her destiny. We are called to build the Kingdom of God and share the Good News of redemption, leading to the conversion and then salvation of souls. That is our destiny.

We must never brush off the place we have in God's plan. How will those we see in our everyday lives come to know the Lord and then find salvation? Mary was the instrument by which the Incarnation came into the world. We are called to be the instruments by which that same Jesus Christ comes into the worlds of those who do not know Him.

References from Wojtyla, Karol. The Word Made Flesh. *San Francisco: Harper & Row, 1985.*

IDEA FOR RESPONSE
Start reading regularly a good Catholic newspaper or magazine, if you already are not doing so.

TAKE TIME TO REFLECT

What are 3 current news stories that were of interest to me? How does my faith affect the way I look at these stories?

DIVINE PLAN

Forsaking Elvis

In the sixth month, the angel Gabriel was sent from God to a town of Galilee called Nazareth, to a virgin betrothed to a man named Joseph, of the house of David, and the virgin's name was Mary. And coming to her, he said, "Hail, favored one! The Lord is with you." But she was greatly troubled at what was said and pondered what sort of greeting this might be. Then the angel said to her, "Do not be afraid, Mary, for you have found favor with God. Behold, you will conceive in your womb and bear a son, and you shall name him Jesus."

—Luke 1:26-31

I heard Mother Dolores, a.k.a. Dolores Hart, speak at the Eucharistic Congress one year in Charlotte, NC. She is often known as the "nun who kissed Elvis." She had a promising career in film and has the notoriety of being cast opposite Elvis Presley in his first movie. But that all changed when she responded to God's call and entered formation for religious life.

She said her response to God's call wasn't easy. She cried herself to sleep many times in the beginning, wondering if she had made the right decision. But as time continued on, she knew that her response would bring her true joy.

Our Lady was not much different than Dolores Hart. We sometimes only focus on the theological reality of her being conceived without original sin and her sinless life. But believing that does not mean we have to believe it was easy. We know Jesus accepted His fate in the Garden of Gethsemane, but Scripture tells us it wasn't easy. And He was God! Mary said yes to the messenger of the Lord, Gabriel, and continued to say yes with the rest of her life. But she was human. Just by being human too, you and I know it could not have been easy.

But mature disciples say yes to God every day, even if that yes will bring hardship and include a heavy cost. Stewardship calls us to stop counting the cost. Each day brings with it a new opportunity for God to place a calling on our heart. Mary one day so long ago said yes to just such a call.

And her "yes" changed the entire history of the human race. Who knows what your next "yes" might mean for the world?

IDEA FOR RESPONSE
Spend 10 minutes in contemplative prayer and just say the name of "Jesus" at each breath inward, and the word "Yes" at each breath outward.

TAKE TIME TO REFLECT
What are 3 things I have said yes to in my life that have made a great impact for the better or made me a better disciple?

YES

Scripture Passages

Notes

Notes

Notes

Notes

Notes

Notes

LOOKING TO CULTIVATE EVERYDAY STEWARDSHIP IN YOUR PARISH COMMUNITY?

Inspiration, Training, Formation, and Leadership Are Key to Creating a Stewardship Parish of Mature Disciples

- ✓ Engagement/Stewardship Workshops & Talks
- ✓ Stewardship Committee/Campaign Consulting
- ✓ Parish Long-Range Planning
- ✓ Parish Stewardship Day for Leaders
- ✓ StrengthsFinder© Coaching and Workshops
- ✓ Parish Missions

For more information, contact Tracy Earl Welliver at (800) 950-9952 ext. 2676 or twelliver@4LPi.com.

About the Author

Tracy Earl Welliver has been a Catholic all his life and is still working hard to truly become an EVERYDAY STEWARD. He is the Director of Parish Community and Engagement for LPi and an active member of Saint Pius X Catholic Church in Greensboro, North Carolina, where he previously served as Pastoral Associate for 22 years. Saint Pius X received the Archbishop Murphy Award in 2009 for excellence in stewardship from the International Catholic Stewardship Council. Tracy is a writer, speaker, and coach in the areas of stewardship, engagement, catechesis, and strengths theory, and has worked with Catholic communities throughout the US, Canada, Australia, and New Zealand.

Tracy writes the blog, The Main Thing, each week with the occasional help from a few of his good friends. You can read Tracy's *Everyday Stewardship* column in LPi's *Connect! Uniting Word & World*, a bimonthly lectionary-based liturgy preparation publication or at *www.tracyearlwelliver.com*. Tracy has theology degrees from DeSales University and Duke Divinity School. He has been married 24 years and he and his wife, Mariann, have 3 children, all of whom serve as constant inspiration for articles and blog posts.

LPi is a stewardship communication company that serves as a single source for products and services that help create more vibrant Catholic faith communities. We offer engagement tools for parishes that include ad-supported church bulletins, websites and newsletters, solutions for digital engagement, including online giving and mobile phone applications.

Recently LPi introduced a line of consulting offerings including a sustainable offertory campaign, stewardship workshops and retreats. Our consultative coaching services and catechesis to help the local church build a stewardship spirituality culture where people actively give back more of their time, treasure and talent in thanks to God for what He has given to them. Our sustainable offertory campaign is designed to help parishes build long-term fiscal discipleship into their community, as well as parish stewardship workshops and retreats to communicate the complete message of stewardship as a way of life.

With a full slate of digital, print, communication and consultative coaching products and services, LPi is helping parishes extend their community and communicate the Good News.

To learn more visit:

BECAUSE VIBRANT CHURCHES MATTER